The God Who Won't Let Go

The God Who Won't Let Go

P<small>ETER</small> <small>VAN</small> B<small>REEMEN</small>, S.J.

ave maria press   Notre Dame, IN

Original publication *Was zaehlt, ist Liebe*. Herder, Freiburg-Basel-Vienna.
Translated from German by the author.
Imprimi potest: The Hague, The Netherlands, Dec. 1, 1998
    Hans van Leeuwen, S.J.
    Provincial of the Dutch Province

www.avemariapress.com

International Standard Book Number: 0-87793-746-X (pb)
                                   0-87793-957-8 (hc)
Cover and text design by Brian C. Conley
Cover photo: www.comstock.com
Printed and bound in the United States of America.

Library of Congress Cataloging-in-Publication Data
Van Breemen, Peter G., 1927- [Was zèahlt, ist Liebe. English]
    The God who won't let go / Peter van Breemen ; [translated from German
by the author].
        p. cm.
    Includes bibliographical references.
    ISBN 0-87793-957-8 -- ISBN 0-87793-746-X
    1. Spiritual life--Catholic Church. 2. Catholic Church--Doctrines.
3. God--Love. I. Title.
    BX2350.3 .V36 2001
    231'.6 dc21
                                                    2001002618
                                                        CIP

Contents

Preface

In March 1998 I spent a week with the Benedictines of St. Hildegard Abbey in Bingen, Germany, guiding them in their annual retreat. Though the present monastery dates from the beginning of the twentieth century, the community itself descends in a direct and uninterrupted line from their first and founding abbess, St. Hildegard, born in 1098. So the year of our retreat was actually the ninth centenary of her birth, marked by numerous scholarly and popular celebrations.

The retreat focused on the basic themes of biblical spirituality. My conferences addressed in the simplest language the depth, rigor, and demands of our Christian faith, while at the same time highlighting the joy, fulfillment, and peace which the gospel is meant to bring. I share these texts, slightly reworked for written publication, with my readers in the hope that these twelve chapters may respond somewhat to the hunger for a genuine, profound, and positive spirituality.

I meet so many people who search for a deeper meaning of life and invest an enormous amount of energy, time, and, yes, money in this search. I am often pained to see how little our Christian tradition connects with this deep yearning, and I wonder what prevents us Christians from being more fully responsive to this obvious and pervasive need of our time. I cannot fully accept the easy explanation that the way of the gospel demands too much commitment and fidelity, because I believe that every honestly searching person wants to be challenged that way. No doubt, we Christians fall short of our ideals; yet, there are enough women and men who live the Christian faith in an authentic and convincing way. Why then can we not render this source of life and fruitfulness more easily accessible? This little book seeks to do just that.

Whoever knows my previous books will recognize not only certain thoughts and topics repeated here in a somewhat different wording and context, but above all the central theme of God's unconditional love for each of us as we are (and not as we should be). God loves us into existence and longs for us to have life and joy in abundance. It is God's abiding desire that our lives be eminently meaningful and bear rich fruit, fruit that lasts. Put simply, what counts is love.

In translating this book from German into English several people helped me greatly and generously, especially two Sisters of Mercy, Marilyn Lacey and Mary Jean Meier. I thank them with all my heart and hope that their efforts will be fruitful, bringing more people closer to our ever-gracious God, source of all life and love.

Peter G. van Breemen, S.J.
Los Angeles, Sept. 15, 1999

ONE

"Wait there for me"

We all seek God. This very moment, if you were not seeking God, you would not have picked up this book. All of us are longing, at the deepest level of our being, for something more, something beyond our comprehension, someone in whom our fulfillment lies. St. John Climacus said, "Happy the person whose longing for God is like the passion of a lover for her beloved."

In all the world's great religions, people seek God. Christianity, however, introduces into the world an unexpected reversal: Christianity reveals a God-who-seeks-us, a God who loves us far more than we love ourselves. Otherwise, how could we exist? God's passionate desire for us, even to the extent that the Word of God became a human being, permeates the whole of sacred scripture and is the *raison d'être* of all creation.

Consider the image that the prophet Hosea, eight centuries prior to the birth of Christ, presents of God seeking us out the way a young man might woo his beloved: "So I will allure her; I will lead her into the desert and speak to her heart" (Hos 2:16). Such warmth and tenderness! This is not a distant, omnipotent deity. Here we see the intimacy of a young lover longing for the girl of his dreams, trying everything possible to get her attention and win her affection. The prophet describes a God who yearns for us, who wants us wholly. Our love matters to God. God will go to any length to seek us out, even if it means leading us into a desert in order to speak directly to our hearts.

In the Song of Songs, we find the same refrain: "I belong to my lover and for me he yearns" (Sg 7:11). Over and over, scripture invites us to believe the startling, wonderful, almost-too-good-to-be-true revelation: *God's longing is for each of us.* Allow yourself to hear the words of scripture, though written long ago, as spoken to you fresh, here and now. Rest in this imagery. Savor it. Dare to address God as Mechtild of Magdeburg once did, "Thou blazing God in thine passionate desire."

Beginning to pray, or deciding to enter more deeply into prayer, means already having made a choice for God. In truth, it means God is already drawing us closer. During times of meditation and contemplation, we renew and deepen our relationship with this God who so wants to be known by us. We can acknowledge this relationship at the outset by praying:

> I marvel at your desire for my company. I stand in awe that your love finds and chooses me, for I had given up all hope of ever being addressed so lovingly by anyone. And now, you choose me and tell me that I make a difference to you! Utterly amazed, I experience myself differently because of your choice. I learn to appreciate myself in a new way. I see my worth and my contribution when I look at myself with your eyes. How can I begin to thank you?

Chapter thirty-four of the book of Exodus relates the encounter of Moses with God on Mt. Sinai. A similar encounter had taken place some time before (cf. Ex 24), but when Moses came down from the mountain he found the people dancing before the golden calf they had fashioned in his absence. Moses's wrath flared up, and he threw down the tablets of the covenant that he had received from God, completely shattering them. Chapter thirty-four, then, begins with the words, "The LORD said to Moses. . . ." Notice that God takes the initiative. God does not abandon Moses to his deep disappointment over the wavering, unruly people. God reaches out again to Moses, just as God's hand stretched out to Adam after the fall, "Where are you?" (Gn 3:9). Though Adam crept away to hide, God took the initiative to renew the contact. It is the same with our prayer. God always takes the first step. God never leaves us alone to our fate, our shame or our guilt. God always invites us toward greater freedom. Even when we ourselves pick and choose the times for meditation, for silence, and for prayer, God is there ahead of us. God has already worked in and through our desires. God is the One who seeks us out. God desires this encounter. In the thirteenth century the Persian poet, Jelaluddin Rumi, voiced this same incredible mystery:

> *Lo, I am with you always,*
> Means when you look for God,
> God is in the look of your eyes,
> in the thought of looking,
> nearer to you than your self,
> or things that have happened to you.[1]

God gave Moses the task to cut two tablets of stone on which God would write the same words that had been engraved on the previous tablets. Here we see another parallel with our own lives: we prepare and open our hearts, but what really counts is done by God. Yes, prayer requires a certain amount of effort and determination on our part, but the deeper action is from God who desires always to console and liberate us. Our faith and our prayer are never just achievements dependent upon our efforts; they are above all letting go, opening up, and making ourselves receptive to God. According to Ignatius of Loyola, the heart of prayer is simply God-at-work-in-us: "Let the Creator deal directly with the creature and the creature directly with the Creator." The most important condition is that we are not in God's way so that God can work freely in us.

When prayer seems lacking in fruitfulness, usually the reason is that we have tried to do too much. Years of experience have convinced me of this. "Doing too much" might mean that we are straining, unwittingly trying to force an experience of God. This only makes us tense, and that tension can then block the gentle movement of God. Doing too much can also mean utilizing the time of prayer for other extraneous activities. After all, we all have so many things to do, and the space reserved for prayer provides splendid opportunities for catching up with other matters. Resist the inclination to make prayer productive. Jesus says that whoever loses her life will find it. Or, more accurately, whoever loses her life for my sake will find it. Similarly, it can be said of prayer that whoever loses her time for Jesus' sake will discover that it becomes the most precious time. Waste your time for Jesus' sake. You will not be disappointed.

With Moses, God wrote on tablets of stone. Later the prophet Jeremiah proclaimed an astonishingly new covenant: "This is the covenant which I will make with the house of Israel after those days, says the LORD. I will place my law within them, and write it upon their hearts; I will be their God, and they shall be my people" (Jer 31:33). St. Paul refers back to Jeremiah's image in 2 Corinthians 3:3, where he addresses his readers (all of us included) as a Letter of Christ, "written not in ink but by the Spirit of the living God, not on tablets of stone but on tablets that are hearts of flesh." There is no need for us to cut and prepare stone tablets, but we must prepare our hearts. The latter could prove more difficult than the former—opening our hearts and keeping them so still that God's word and God's message can be imprinted there. To pray always means to stand before God with an open heart and open hands.

I like the image of the open hands. Over the years, we have all gathered a great deal in our hands—perhaps with great effort—and naturally we want to hold onto all of it. We hold modern conveniences that make our lives easier. We cling to convictions and opinions, thoughts and ideas. We treasure relationships, of course. And we hold in our hands work, appointments, calendar, position, reputation, influence, and so much more. We hold on. We are not willing to give them up lightly. We have expended considerable energy accumulating all these precious things.

When we pray, we open our hands. It is not necessary to empty them. The point is simply to remain before God with our hands wide open, waiting. God also shows much patience. After some time God may come and look lovingly at what we hold. "You have a lot," God says. Yes, we answer, that is certainly true. We have much, probably much more than even we ourselves realize. Then God may look at us directly and ask, "Is it all right with you if I take this out?" Do not be afraid. God is gentle. God can never harm. You can be sure of that. On the other hand, God knows how to choose. The fundamental stance of prayer remains, "Yes, you may take whatever you choose." We can agree because we know that God loves us more than we love ourselves and that God would never take anything if it were to harm us.

After God has taken that one thing, we remain in God's presence. If after a while God comes again, we may feel a bit nervous. God asks, "Is it all right if I put this in your hand and entrust it to you?" God never takes without also giving. Once again, the bottom line in our prayer is, "Yes, you may." Without this basic attitude, we cannot really pray. Our entire relationship with God would slip into an exercise of "hide and seek." We seek God, but when we find ourselves close to God, we withdraw for fear that God might take something away. So prayer becomes literally impossible if we refuse to let

God be God. If that desire is lacking, prayer cannot be authentic. Rabindranath Tagore captured it succinctly when he wrote, "There is an anguish in my heart for the burden of its riches not given to you." Whatever we withhold from God burdens us.

Nevertheless, it would be a serious mistake to begin conjecturing as to what God might conceivably take from our hands. Don't do that! It would only lead in the wrong direction. We could all imagine a thousand things, but what God is really going to ask of us, we won't discover that way. God is far too original and too surprising for that. Besides, we should not be focusing on our hands and what we hold; that is not the point of prayer. Our eyes should be on God alone, and with boundless confidence. When God desires to take something from our hands, it is invariably because God desires that we become more truly ourselves. God is more faithful to us than we are to ourselves. We may at times be wary of ourselves, but we never have reason to be afraid of God. Prayer springs from confidence in God who loves us, who desires our growth and well-being. "I came so that they might have life and have it more abundantly" (Jn 10:10). What we need is openness before God, the openness of trust.

One of St. Augustine's homilies contains this insight: "The Word of God opposes your will only until it becomes the author of your salvation. As long as you are your own enemy, the Word of God is also your enemy. Be your own friend, then the Word of God will agree with you." We have nothing to fear. To pray is to open up for God, to grow in the desire that God enter more and more into our lives. Even that misses the mark, because God already dwells in our hearts. Ruysbroec, a fourteenth century Flemish mystic, wrote, "God is the one who approaches us from inside outwards." Truly, God is closer to us than we are to ourselves. Occasionally we are not true to ourselves, not authentic. But God remains faithful always, without exception. God cannot *not* love us.

"Morning after morning he opens my ear that I may hear" (Is 50:4). Other translations say "that I may listen like a disciple." What does it mean to *listen like a disciple*? We may be more naturally inclined to listen like *teachers*, checking to see if other persons have understood us. Prayer reverses that stance: we are called to listen like disciples, like learners. We are invited to open ourselves before God-who-reveals.

Perhaps we view prayer time as pleasant. Meditation, after all, can create a sense of tranquility, bringing refreshment to the spirit and affirmation to the heart. But this understanding falls far short of the real experience of prayer. Such thinking shows that our image of God remains far too small. Time and time again it happens that one experiences a breakthrough in prayer. Many people have experienced this further invitation to enter into a deeper intimacy with God. It may occur to us, too, and it might occur more than once in our lives. The classic example comes from the life of St. Teresa of Avila who, after nineteen years in a mediocre Carmel—a place neither bad nor really good—experienced God directly. In the years prior, Teresa herself had lived a lukewarm life, neither fervent nor apathetic. *That* Teresa would never have had a place in history. With her conversion the saint was born and she has borne tremendous fruit for the church even to the present day.

We find another example in Gertrud of Helfta. She could indicate exactly the time and place in the dormitory where she was liberated from an idol. The idol was her excessive love for scholarship. In that moment, she opened her hands. Then the love of God really seized her and set her on the path to holiness.

This same God is also at work in our lives, and not only during prayer. Such life-changing experiences continue to happen today. God is always greater than we think. Expect to be surprised by love beyond imagining. Each day is full of fresh possibility. Each day God wakes us to listen like disciples.

After God had spoken to Moses, giving him the task of cutting two tablets of stone, God added one more instruction: "Be ready at dawn; at dawn come up Mount Sinai and wait for me there at the top of the mountain" (Ex 34:2, NJB).

Wait for me there! The essence of prayer is not our searching for God, because that can easily become too active, but rather our waiting, our letting go, our bearing with our own inadequacy. Waiting for someone is a very authentic way of honoring that person, more authentic perhaps than any words we might speak or gifts we might offer. In waiting we experience our own powerlessness. Waiting does not come easily. However, we cannot force God. God will come, there is no doubt about that, but in God's own time. Therefore, *wait for me there!* This waiting is not empty, dead time. We wait because there is already a relationship. We wait for Someone.

"No one shall come up with you, and no one is even to be seen on any part of the mountain; even the flocks and the herds are not to go grazing toward this mountain" (Ex 34:3). God wants Moses's complete attention. God's love allows no compromises.

"Moses then cut two stone tablets like the former, and early the next morning he went up Mount Sinai as the LORD had commanded him, taking along the two stone tablets. Having come down in a cloud, the LORD stood with him there and proclaimed his name, 'LORD'" (Ex 34:4-5). Notice that it is not Moses who calls on the Lord, but God who proclaims God's own name. That is to say, God makes himself known. Here is the real secret of experiencing God: that God—to a certain extent—reveals God's own self. That is what counts. Nothing we do can approximate this experience.

The desert fathers and mothers compare the experience of praying with the situation of hounds who chase a hare.[2] One dog spots the hare; then it barks excitedly and starts running. Other dogs hear the barking and join in the chase. But sooner or later, the dogs who only heard the barking give up. Those who have seen the hare, however, keep running. It is an apt image for our prayer: whoever prays only because he has heard the barking of others without seeing anything himself will not persevere.

This analogy describes the pain of many honest seekers. They live on the "barking" of others, and in the long run that is simply not enough. They search for the meaning of life, for inner peace, ultimately for God (named or not), but they only hear from someone else who heard that someone heard, and so on. Of course, we cannot bring about an experience of God through our own efforts. Such can only be given to us. It is sheer gift. But when we wait with open hands and unde-fended heart, God does come. We do experience God's pres-ence. We have God's word on it! "When you look for me, you will find me. Yes, when you seek me with all your heart, you will find me with you, says the LORD" (Jer 29:13-14). St. Augustine wrote in his *Confessions*, "Say to me in the fullness of your mercy, my Lord and my God, who you are for me. Say to my soul, I am your salvation. Say it in such a way that I hear and understand" (Conf. I. 5, 5). This is what prayer is all about: that we hear the Word of God and find our fulfillment there.

"Moses at once bowed down to the ground in worship" (Ex 34:8). We know how integral our body is to everything we do; prayer is no exception. Spirituality that attempts to be dis-embodied is certainly not Christian spirituality. We seek God as whole persons. Our longing and reverence for God naturally express themselves in gesture, as scripture often notes. But it also works the other way around. The posture of the body influences the attitude of the mind. Awareness of the interaction can be quite helpful. What we need is a pos-ture of the body that expresses genuine reverence for the presence of the Holy One, yet is at the same time relaxed enough not to absorb our attention. In times of desolation, when "the well runs dry," body posture can still give shape to our deepest desires.

Finally the Lord says to Moses (Ex 34:10), "Here, then . . . is the covenant I will make." Again, Moses's experience parallels the prayer into which God invites each of us. On the one hand, Moses waits on the top of the mountain all by himself, in com-plete solitude and silence. On the other hand, the covenant that God offers in the midst of that solitude is not a covenant between God and Moses, but rather between God and *the people*. Out of Moses's solitary experience of God there emerges something of great importance for all the people. Similarly, we pray alone, in solitude and silence; but—and this is good to remember when prayer happens to be difficult—our solitary prayer bears fruit for many. We wait by ourselves, but our listening, our silence, our longing, and our prayer become a source of fruitfulness for others as well. This fruitfulness knows no bounds.

Good, giver of life
you alone know
how our life can truly succeed.
Teach us in the silence of your presence
to reverence this mystery:
how in the encounter with you,
how under your gaze and in your word
we recognize ourselves
as your image and likeness.
Show us how to let go
of whatever hinders us
from meeting you,
from letting ourselves be touched by your
    Word.
Help us to welcome and accept
whatever in us yearns to come alive
in the image and likeness
you have dreamed for us
today and every day
for ever and ever.[3]

Two

We all need more love than we deserve

Among many long, complicated sentences in a book by the German philosopher Jorg Splett, I found this simple gem, "Every person needs more love than he or she deserves." How clear. How true. No scholarly language is needed to explain this, but it is nonetheless profound. When we read this little sentence, all kinds of people come to our mind to confirm it: people who need more love than they deserve. Perhaps you think of an undocumented alien or a homeless person or a drug addict. But you don't have to go beyond the circle of your own acquaintances. In your own surroundings, in your nearest neighborhood, you will find people who need more love than they deserve. Upon deeper reflection, something of the spirit of the Sermon on the Mount can grow in us, a certain kindliness and mercy which every community needs.

This statement also applies much closer to home. It describes me. I am such a person! I myself need more love than I deserve. In order to delve into this sentence more deeply, notice that it really states two truths: first, that I need love; and secondly, more of it than I deserve.

I need love! Every person is gifted with many talents. Nature is not thrifty in spreading new seeds of life; on the contrary, it does so lavishly. In the same way, God is not stingy in bestowing gifts on us. Think of the intellect and its enormous potential, which is indeed a very precious talent. But it is only one of many. There are the talents of the hands—creative people who can design or fix anything. That too is a special talent. Then there are also gifts of the heart, such as empathy, mercy, and genuine respect, and in the long run they are even more important than all the others. If we take the word "talent" in this broad sense, we can truly say that every person has many talents.

Just as in nature, so it is with us: our talents need an appropriate climate in order to thrive. As long as the weather is bleak or cold, the buds of the flowers and the trees remain closed because it would be too risky for them to open up. But when spring approaches, bringing warmer weather, they open up and gladden us with an array of flowers and foliage. So it is with ourselves. When the atmosphere in which we live remains frosty or unwelcoming, we do not dare to really open ourselves. Under such conditions, the talents we have remain hidden and closed.

In Berlin, where the closing time of shops is very strictly regulated, I once had to buy something in a supermarket on a Friday evening shortly before the store would close. All but one of the counters had already shut down. The one which was still open had a long line of customers, most of whom looked decidedly impatient and annoyed because the other counters had closed too early. I noticed, however, that the people at the very front of the line seemed to be in a good mood. I thought it was because they were about to be served. That certainly was one reason, but I soon discovered that there was a second reason. The checker had made a sign out of a piece of cardboard and put it in front of her. It said, "We have been made with love; please treat us accordingly." With this simple message, she transformed irritated tempers into friendly smiles. We need such reminders.

In a bold sweeping vision, the German theologian and cultural historian, Eugen Biser, reduces the troubles of the present generation to three basic problems: over-activity, loneliness, and *angst*. In a world in which these few basic problems shape the climate, we sorely need the message of the checker so that the atmosphere becomes warmer and more relaxed. The poet Pablo Neruda expresses it with a lovely image, "I would like to do with you what spring does with a cherry tree."

Our spirits need love just as much as our bodies need air. Only then do the untold possibilities dormant within us come to life and fruition. When we love and are loved, our loneliness is transformed into intimacy, our angst into courage, and, as in Jacob's dream (Gn 28:10-19), the gateway to heaven opens up. In *Amazing Grace*, Kathleen Norris relates a simple but striking experience.

> One morning this past spring I noticed a young couple with an infant at an airport departure gate. The baby was staring intently at other people, and as soon as he recognized a human face, no matter whose it was, no matter if it was young or old, pretty or ugly, bored or happy or worried-looking, he would respond with absolute delight. It was beautiful to see. Our drab departure gate had become the gate of heaven. And as I watched that baby play with any adult who would allow it, I felt as awe-struck as Jacob, because I realized that this is how God looks at us, staring into our faces in order to be delighted, to see the creature he made and called good, along with the rest of creation. . . . I suspect that only God, and well-loved infants, can see this way.[1]

Jesus tells us, "By this is my Father glorified, that you bear much fruit and become my disciples" (Jn 15:8). God wants our lives to be worthwhile. God's plan is that we bear fruit, fruit in abundance. In that way God is glorified. Yes, God glories in such a life! In the next verse Jesus reveals the secret of that rich fruitfulness, "As the Father loves me, so I also love you. Remain in my love."

There we find the axis of a fruitful life: staying connected with Jesus in the love between Father and Son. There we blossom and bear fruit. To remain in that love involves more than just thinking of it occasionally. To remain in that love means that the love of God is our home, our security, our joy. Only in this way does our life truly flourish.

The seventeenth-century Austrian priest-poet, Angelus Silesius, dared to sum it up this way: "Nothing or no one is more beautiful than I, since God—beauty itself—has fallen in love with me." This is exactly what Jesus desires—that we know and realize how precious we are in God's eyes, that God allures us and speaks to our heart, that it means very much to God to gain our love. An ancient Jewish maxim says: "Before every human being comes a retinue of angels announcing, 'Make way for an image of the Holy One, Blessed be God.'" Out of the same tradition: "Don't think little of yourself, because God does not think little of you." Ask God for the gift of seeing yourself as God sees you—beloved beyond all measure.

I need love, however—and now it becomes intriguing—more than I deserve. My own achievements are not sufficient. We live in an achievement-crazed society in which everything has to be earned. If my own accomplishments are less than my needs, then I am in trouble! Yet we all need more love than we deserve. That "more" must be granted as a gift. We call that grace. Everything hinges on that "more." Even of greater importance is that we accept the more when it is given. If it is offered but not accepted, our life remains under the yoke of inadequacy. Truly, the greatest difficulty may lie in the accepting. Have we not learned that it is more blessed to give than to receive? (see Acts 20:35). And have we not, therefore, been trained in giving rather than in receiving? Especially, are not most of us quite unprepared for accepting a love which we do not deserve?

There is yet another difficulty. We all know that the word love has many meanings. For some, love is primarily romantic; for others, love is primarily physical; still others interpret love as selflessness; some strive for purely spiritual love which leaves behind the world's hustle and bustle. Love, however, has not only many meanings, but also several shapes. There is the love between husband and wife, the love of parents for their children, and of children for their parents. There is love in religious communities and in parish communities. There is love among friends. There are many forms of love!

Jean Vanier, founder of L'Arche communities, points to the core when he describes love as "revealing to someone else that person's own beauty." Love means showing the other how beautiful he or she is. The other person cannot discover this alone; even a mirror will not suffice. Another human being is needed. Where that happens, love is realized.

Faith and love intertwine. And like love, faith roots itself in the exigencies of our daily lives. There are points of contact with psychology—all that I have experienced in my own life shapes, to a certain extent, my faith. There is a connection between faith and sociology: I do not become a believer in isolation but only in community, in contact and exchange with others. My faith in this way is also affected by church politics.

John touches the heart of our faith when he writes in his first letter: "We have come to know and to believe in the love God has for us" (1 Jn 4:16). Believing in the love God has for us, according to John, is the essence of our faith. This love which God has for us is not abstract but deeply personal; not a general principle, but a bold, creative affection for each of us as we are (and not as we feel we should be).

To believe genuinely stretches not only our image of God but also our sense of self. Some people may accept God's love in general, but balk as soon as it becomes personal. "Of course God loves everyone, but not me. I am the exception." This attitude most likely bespeaks a poignant pain stemming from not having been accepted or loved by others. Genuine faith is always intensely personal. We ought not to underestimate how difficult it is to believe that in our uniqueness, we are loved by God unconditionally. This, precisely, is the gift we call "faith." We cannot achieve this on our own. Faith is always a gift of our gracious God.

A recent French book on the psalms called faith "the shuddering certainty of love."[2] Yes, faith is certain of love. But not a certainty that can be taken for granted. Faith is literally awe-filled, so profound that it pushes us to the edge of disbelief. We tremble because of our unworthiness, emotion, and wonder. We struggle with a measure of resistance: this cannot be right. It does not apply to me, does not agree with my life history. It seems too stunning to be true: I am utterly beloved of God. In the words of Macrina Wiederkehr, "O God, help me to believe the truth about myself, no matter how beautiful!" Accepted and taken seriously, faith turns our lives around. Believing in this awesome love that God has for me, I stand amazed and immensely grateful. How can this be? Is it really true? Am I so loved?

This is our faith. God loves me into existence. Out of God's love I come forth, not only once at my birth but every day and at every moment. God's love for me is the ever-renewed and inexhaustible source of my life.

For many years I wrestled with a pastoral problem. I still have not resolved it, but I am gradually coming to understand it better. Often I pondered people who cannot believe that God's love goes out to them personally. We have all known persons who were not happy in their childhood. At home they did not experience much affection or warmth; they had to live up to stringent expectations; they had to earn the love of their parents with high grades and good behavior, and when the marks remained below par, the reaction would be harsh. The child felt punished. Some experienced far worse: people who were sexually abused as a child, perhaps by relatives, sometimes even by one of their parents. Of course, these people can have the greatest difficulty believing in God's love. That love is in no way self-evident for them. On the contrary, the very idea of such love meets with a wall of bitter or angry resistance: that cannot be true, that is not real, that is not in tune with their lives. How can these people ever come to believe the gospel as good news?

Only very slowly did I find an approach to this burning question. In theology there is a school of thought, shared among others by Karl Barth and Dietrich Bonhoeffer, that strongly emphasizes God as completely different: the Wholly Other. This theology has a very long tradition which goes back to the first centuries of Christianity. It is called the apophatic or negative theology. It holds that we can never adequately speak about God with our human experiences and concepts. The mystics have always deeply experienced this truth, that God is entirely Other. This is especially true when we attempt to speak of God's love. The love of God differs radically, entirely, from all human love which we have ever experienced. In order to believe genuinely in *God's* love we need to make a quantum leap of faith.

We have to leap from our experiences of human love into the totally other realm of God's love. This analogy of the faith leap has, of course, its limitations. The image may create the impression that we have to make this jump only once, and then we will have arrived on the other side. The reality is not so simple; we have to jump again and again.

Faith makes this huge leap into the unknown territory of divine love. A person who in his or her early years was unhappy in the experience—or rather lack of experience—of human love needs much courage and strength to risk this leap. But no one is exempt from leaping! Even those whose childhoods were blessed with much affection in harmonious families must learn to leap. Such persons, however, might tend to stall, refuse to jump, and settle for believing that divine love is just like what they experienced at home, but a bit fuller. Whoever thinks that way does not yet believe in the full sense of the word. Everyone has to make the leap. Who can say for whom the leap is easier or more difficult? Both starting points have their own specific difficulties. One person lacks any experiential grounding in human love, but at the same time longs for something more meaningful and joyful than what she experienced so far. The other person has much to be grateful for, but is called not to constrain God's love to his own limited experience. For each person, astounding grace lies in the leaping: love beyond that which we could ever ask or imagine; unconditional love already given.

God's love is completely different from all human love. God's love is unconditional, it does not even put the condition that we exist. In fact, God loved us before we existed. Human love is always limited and conditional. God's love is not so at all, but radically different.

God's love is based on nothing. That may sound somewhat disappointing. We prefer to think: God loves me because I am so dedicated and unselfish or because of my personality, my special qualities. When we are told that God's love does not depend on those "things," the very natural and legitimate question arises, "Does the love of God, then, go out to *me*?" The answer is an unqualified *yes*. You, in the singular uniqueness of your personality, different from all others, are loved by God with an unconditional love and an inconceivably great fidelity and earnestness. But you did absolutely nothing to arouse, elicit, or earn this love of God. It was there before you existed. God's love is based on nothing! Let us be very grateful for this truth. If God's love were based on something and this something broke down, then the whole structure would collapse. But we are sure that this cannot happen, precisely because God's love is based on nothing.

Ruysbroec speaks of "the bottomless love of God." No matter how deeply we are immersed in God's love, we never reach the bottom, since that does not exist. God's love has no limit, no end. Trying to imagine this we become dizzy. Our imagination is too limited. We cannot conceive of something without boundaries. A border always appears somewhere in our imagination. Perhaps there is still something beyond that border, but we cannot imagine it without the border. God's love is unlimited, bottomless, without any boundary. It is sheer surprise. It is the very root and the absolute origin. God's love is solid and firm and absolutely reliable.

Peter Knauer articulated this truth in a terse yet precise way: "God takes the measure of his love not on us, but on Himself." That is another way to say that God's love is wholly other. We measure our love by the other person. That is why we love one person more and another less. It all depends on the personality of the other and the limits of my affection. God, however, does not measure love by any standard. God's love has no limits. Would someone say: "God begins here and ends there"? God loves because God is Love. We *do* love, whereas God *is* love.

"In our creation we had a beginning, but the love in which God created us, was in God without beginning" (Julian of Norwich). The love from which we come forth is eternal and encompasses us completely, including our shadow, our inadequacies, and yes, our failures. The Book of Wisdom goes one step further:

> For even if we sin, we are yours, and know
> your might;
> but we will not sin, knowing that we belong
> to you (Wis. 15:2).

Even when we sin, God's love continues to carry us. This is unthinkable. To sin means to refuse God's love. But when we deny God's love, that love still remains and does not let us down. None of us can ever claim to understand this. We can reject the love which is the origin of our life, and yet live on. We can, so to speak, saw off the branch on which we sit, and yet not fall. Don't try that with a tree in your garden or in the woods! But with God, this is possible. Even in our sins, God does not let us down. In our finitude we are infinitely loved by

God. This love reaches to the root of our existence, further and deeper than all our limitations and idiosyncrasies. God's love does not depend on our being this way or that. God's love is our origin and our home. Jesus invites us to remain there always.

Karl Rahner closed a Christmas sermon with words which provide a good summary of this chapter, and can enrich our personal prayer:

> God has entrusted his last, deepest, and most beautiful word to the world, in the Word made flesh. This Word says: I love you world, man and woman. I am there. I am with you. I am your life. I am your time. I weep your tears. I am your joy. Do not be afraid. When you do not know how to go any further, I am with you. I am in your anguish, because I suffered it myself. I am in your need and your death, because today I began to live and to die with you. I am your life. I promise you: for you, too, life is waiting. For you, too, the gates will open.[3]

Y ou nourish and sustain the world
from day to day,
and wherever we go
you are present more fully
than we dare presume.
We thank you for this presence,
this hidden, vulnerable,
yet faithful presence here and now.
We believe in it and live from you
as we live from bread,
as we hunger and thirst for peace,
today and every day for ever and ever.[4]

THREE

Source of our freedom

We all know the words of Jesus, "the truth will set you free" (Jn 8:32). As a student, I was fascinated by this promise. I understood it to mean that whoever studies much and accumulates vast amounts of knowledge, can move more freely in this world. Precisely that study taught me later that the word "truth" in John's gospel has quite a different meaning from what I thought originally.

Whenever the word "truth" occurs in scripture, it always goes back to the Hebrew word "emeth." This word is difficult to translate since it stems from a completely different culture. It might be helpful first to have a quick look at the symbol that expresses the meaning of the word *emeth*. That symbol is the rock. On rock one can build. Rock is firm and solid. *Emeth* in scripture signifies the utmost reliability. If we translate the word *emeth* with truth—and that is common—then it has to be understood in the sense of an existential truth rather than an intellectual truth. *Emeth* is truth on which one can build one's existence, the foundation that is steady and stable. The word "amen," by the way, has the same root as *emeth* and expresses a strong and heartfelt approval: so it is!

Around 1950 Father Augustin Bea, who later became a cardinal, was the rector of the Biblicum in Rome. Pope Pius XII entrusted him with preparing a new Latin translation of the

Psalms. Instead of using the usual translation of *emeth* with *veritas* (truth), Father Bea selected the word *fidelity*. In his opinion, *fidelity* better conveys what the Hebrew word *emeth* implies. Of course, this too is only an attempt. A concept so essential and basic cannot simply be transferred into another language by just one word, because a whole world of culture and religion resonate in it.

Emeth comes close to the unconditional love of God, which is the absolute foundation of our life. It is the love of God which I cannot earn since it was there before I even existed. Nor can I lose it no matter how evil my behavior may be, since that love is everlasting. I do, however, have the choice to accept or reject this love. But even when I reject it, it still remains. That was what I meant in the previous chapter when I talked about the branch on which one sits and saws off without falling down.

In chapter three of Exodus, the Divine Name *par excellence* is revealed, the name Yahweh (YHWH). It is the sacred name, so holy that no Orthodox Jew will ever pronounce it. Its meaning, "I Am Who Am," forever remains unfathomable. God's name, like God's very being, remains mysterious, a unique balance of nearness and distance. It is significant that God reveals his name in the context of liberation. The name, "I Am Who Am," guarantees God's presence and establishes our freedom. The name calls us to live as an image and a partner and a co-worker of "I Am Who Am," with regard to both God and our neighbor. This name is for us a promise and a mission. It is our task to accept and live this presence and freedom, and this constitutes an enormous challenge.

In 1939 Erich Fromm published a book under the title, *Escape From Freedom*. In his foreword the author explained that the book was not really finished, but that circumstances forced him to publish it anyway. These circumstances, he makes clear, were the rise of National Socialism which he rightly considered a terrible threat. In this book he gives a brilliant analysis of the psychology of this movement. He summarizes its basic ideology in one line: to kick the inferior and to flatter the superior.

Christian freedom means the exact opposite. We are called to stoop down to the poor and needy and to behave frankly and with genuine self-respect towards our superiors (and all others as well). The freedom of the gospel means attention, respect, and willingness to help the vulnerable, the poor, and the marginalized: "Amen, I say to you, whatever you did for one of these least brothers [or sisters] of mine, you did for me" (Mt 25:40). At the same time this freedom is characterized by a sound self-esteem, a proper sense of self-worth, and a fearlessness with regards to those in authority: "I no longer call you slaves, . . . I have called you friends" (Jn 15:15).

This freedom is given to us without our deserving it, but not for nothing. It is meant to be lived. Alfred Delp, S.J. wrote shortly before he was hanged by the Nazis in Berlin, "The origin of human freedom lies in the encounter with God." Yes, in the encounter with God human freedom is born.

It may sound strange, but the Old Testament really starts with the third chapter of the Book of Exodus. Exodus 3, not Genesis 1, marks the beginning of the Bible. In that chapter the exodus of the Israelites from Egypt begins. This momentous event transformed a throng of slaves laboring under Pharaoh's rule into a nation, the chosen people of God. The transformation occurred in a tremendous experience of God, an unforgettable encounter with the power of the Most High reflected upon by later generations. After this experience of liberation from slavery in Egypt, Israel went back in time, so to speak, to understand more deeply their faith in YHWH. Israel then discovered that this God, "I Am Who Am," who liberated them from bondage is, in fact, the God of the whole world, the Creator of the universe. The account of the Garden of Eden (Gn 2) and of the fall of Adam and Eve (Gn 3) was actually written five centuries after the exodus from Egypt. The story of creation (Gn 1) comes another two centuries later. After the exodus, Israel reflected backwards in time. The prophet Isaiah captured this evolution in one verse,

Thus says the LORD, your redeemer,
　　who formed you from the womb:
I am the LORD, who made all things,
　　who alone stretched out the heavens;
　　when I spread out the earth, who was
　　with me? (Is 44:24).

This one verse contains it all. First speaks the Lord, your redeemer, who redeemed and liberated you. Then God asserts that God formed you from the womb; so God is not only your redeemer but also your creator. And then, God is not only *your* creator, but the Maker of all things.

Freedom is an integral part of human dignity and rights. People pray and fight, suffer and even die for their freedom. In the course of human history many wars of liberation have been fought, and they continue today. On a smaller scale, we all witness similar "wars" in families, in communities, and in the church whenever human freedom and dignity is at stake. There also exist caricatures and misconceptions about the true meaning of freedom. A confrere who worked many years in Indonesia as a missionary once told me that the people in Jakarta (in those days called Batavia) expected that they would not have to pay anymore for the streetcar after their liberation from Dutch colonial rule, since they would be free now. That turned out to be a misunderstanding of freedom. They underestimated their own responsibility for the greater good of the whole society.

In our own personal lives, misconceptions of the true meaning of freedom also occur. If we observe with sincerity and self-criticism what goes on in us beneath the surface, we soon discover that the greatest dangers to freedom do not come from the outside, but from the inside. The worst tyrants live in our own hearts. Many a freedom in the long run turns out to be an addiction of one kind or another. Once we realize this, we understand that the struggle for freedom will be a lifelong struggle with ourselves. It is a long way to become a free person. St. Paul writes,

> even though there are so-called gods in heaven and on earth (there are, to be sure, many "gods" and many "lords"), yet for us there is one God, the Father,
> from whom all things are and for whom we exist,
> and one Lord, Jesus Christ,
> through whom all things are and through whom we exist (1 Cor 8:5-6).

Yes, there are many gods and lords from whom we have to liberate ourselves. God calls us to do so and guarantees that it can be done.

We struggle to attain this freedom for ourselves, and then must give it freely to others as well. What matters is not so much the freedom we claim for us and for our group, but rather the freedom we allow others and their groups. These two forms of freedom are intimately connected.

Before Moses sets out for the great adventure of liberating his people from Egypt, he receives a sign from God, "I will be with you; and this shall be your sign that it is I who sent you: when you bring my people out of Egypt you shall worship God on this very mountain" (Ex 3:12, *NRSV*). In general, a sign functions only within a relationship. This is because a sign is by nature ambiguous; it can always be interpreted in various ways. The closer the relationship, the greater the ability to pick up what the sign really wants to express. That is why mothers and lovers are such experts in "picking up signals"—that is, perceiving and interpreting signs. With God it is likewise. The signs which God gives can only be understood within the context of faith in the living God; otherwise, they are meaningless. The worship of God on Mount Sinai is proclaimed by "I Am Who Am" as a sign of God's presence and liberating intervention. Adoration opens us for God's working and thus makes us free.

In his book *The Lord*, Romano Guardini poses the question, "Can the spirit become ill?"—not the psyche or the mind, but the spirit. He answers his own question in the affirmative; it can happen when the relationship to the truth becomes muddled. If a person does not deal truthfully with the truth, the spirit becomes ill. That is far worse than a physical or psychic illness. He also asks whether a sick spirit can be cured. And once again he answers affirmatively; the healing takes place in adoration, because in adoration the relationship to the truth is clarified. In adoration the heart is renewed in truth, relationships are set right again, and the spirit is purified. In adoration we let God be God.

A fourth-century hymn prays to Christ, "O, You our Physician, heal our freedom. May it be sanctified and blessed by you. Do not tire to help our freedom, because its healing depends on you." Someone who prays in this way knows how endangered our freedom is. This holds true not only in the fourth century, but also in the twenty-first.

The ten commandments are mentioned twice in scripture: in Exodus 20 and in Deuteronomy 5. When we learned them by heart as children, we began with the words, "I am the Lord Thy God . . ." and then followed the ten commandments, ten injunctions. We memorized them like stern commands from the highest authority. However, if we look carefully at what scripture says, we are in for a surprise. The ten commandments stand completely in the context of freedom. They begin in this way, "I, the LORD am your God, who brought you out of the land of Egypt, that place of slavery" (Ex 20:2). I liberated you. And I want you to be free and to become more and more free. That is why I give you ten basic directives for your lasting and ever-growing freedom.

The ten commandments are the Magna Carta of freedom. They proclaim solemnly that God is the origin and the guarantor of our freedom. They explain what freedom really entails, from God's perspective. They declare freedom as gift and task, grace and command. Let us now consider them, one by one, from God's point of view.

The first commandment: You shall be free if you do not equate anything with God. God provides the all-encompassing guidance for your life. If you let God be God, then you are a free person. If you adore God, all else will be relative, in the double sense of the word. All the rest will be brought into relationship with God. Everything will be seen in connection with God. We shall delight in finding God in everything and everything in God. But also in the other meaning of the word: everything becomes relative, comparative, and loses its absoluteness. If you worship and adore God, then the priorities of your life fall into the right order. Only then can we make responsible choices. In this way clarity, transparency, and freedom enter our lives.

The second commandment: You will be free if you trust the name of God, "I Am Who Am," or "I am there for you." Then you will experience that God sets you free when you are confined, kindles light in your darkness, and delivers you from your anguish. The name of God opens the gate to life. Know that God will appear in your life—often, in surprising ways, and each time differently! You cannot capture God in an image. Therefore, you are not supposed to make a picture of God. If you confine God to an image, you will bypass the living God without even noticing! If you create a portrait of God, you are no longer open for the genuine encounter with the living God. God's best name, Brother David Steindl-Rast contends, is "Surprise."

The third commandment: Observe the sabbath and keep it holy. You shall be free if you can accept that achievements and success are not ultimates in life. Don't let yourself be defined by others, neither by their praise nor by their criticism. You bear the divine within yourself where you are loved and respected by God unconditionally. In this inner core of your being, you can find a peace which others can neither give you nor take away.

Many people, regrettably, measure their worth by their accomplishments: I am what I achieve. Such is our world and, sadly, even our church. Achievements guarantee us a reputation. We Christians maintain that the most important element in our life is our relationship with God, our faith and prayer, and especially our love. But in reality, the good ones are those who accomplish a lot. And who does not like to be a good one? Yet basing our worth on our achievements costs us dearly. The Sabbath commandment seeks to prevent precisely such loss. Your life carries infinitely greater worth than your achievements. Do not be defined by achievements, because the adoration of idols leads inevitably to ruin. Rather, take time out regularly to celebrate the gift of God which we call life. Enjoy Sabbath as a day of rest in the Lord. Pope John XXIII used to say to himself, "Don't take yourself so seriously!" And then, he would go to sleep.

The fourth commandment: Honor your father and your mother, that you may have a long life in the land which the Lord, your God, is giving you. You shall be free if you can be grateful for what your parents gave you, if you can entrust yourself to the origin of your life, if you can accept yourself with your past and with all that your past did with you. Undoubtedly it is of paramount importance that your parents accept you as you are, but it is also vital that you accept your parents as they are or were. They, too, are people who need more love than they deserve. As long as you do not accept them, you cannot fully unfold. Many people have difficulties with their parents, finding fault with their philosophy of life, their interpretation of the faith, their education, or the atmosphere in the family, not to mention far worse things. The way to reconciliation and healing can be long and hard. But as adult persons we cannot shirk this effort, for our parents' sake and for our own. Often enough reconciliation with our parents gives rise to more self-acceptance and peace with our own life history. That releases great energy.

The fifth commandment: You shall not kill. You shall be free if you can accept the life of others as gift. Do not consider them rivals or competitors whom you seek to outdo, but discover in the uniqueness of the other an enrichment to treasure. Never forget that everything lethal stems from a jealous heart. Envy is a threat to life. The great Teresa of Avila said, "Comparing is the death of the spiritual life." She puts it very strongly. She does not say that it is *harmful* for the spiritual life, but that it is the *end* of the spiritual life! Then it is finished. You can still go to church or wear a cross, but your spiritual life is dead. Whoever compares focuses no longer on God, but squints toward the other, leading either to discontent and discouragement or to presumption and arrogance. Such a person is no longer centered, no longer one with God.

The sixth commandment: You shall not commit adultery. You shall be free if you can love people without taking advantage of them. Never use another person as a means for your own plans or ends. Do not bind people to yourself, but help them find their grounding in God. Do not usurp them. Respect is the heart of love.

The seventh commandment: You shall not steal. Whoever clings to something or someone is not free. You shall be free and be able to appreciate without envy the gifts and possessions of others if you can thank God wholeheartedly for the goods and gifts of the other person. Possessions do not render you free. Freedom arises in the letting go, time and time again, so that you are not possessed by things. Make a habit of being grateful. Gratitude makes us free.

The eighth commandment: You shall not bear false witness against your neighbor. You shall be free if you are guileless. "The truth will set you free" (Jn 8:32); truth here understood in the sense of truthfulness. Lying destroys trust. If our life becomes a cunning lie, we destroy our own happiness. Insincerity entangles us in an ever-more complicated net of fallacies. It confines us behind façades that become increasingly unstable. In this way we waste much energy and never find true peace. The more transparent we become, the more we radiate happiness.

The ninth commandment: You shall not covet your neighbor's wife. You shall be free when you can accept existing connections and relationships. Do not try to impose yourself on others or to buy into friendships. We can long for friendship, but we cannot *make* it. If we are preoccupied with a friendship, we may destroy it because in that case we turn the inner gift outward, wrenching what is meant to simply *be* into something we try to grasp. The experience of genuine love is always an undeserved gift.

The tenth commandment: You shall not covet your neighbor's house . . . or anything that belongs to him. You shall be free if deep down in your heart you are content. Concupiscence stems from a heart obsessed by an inner urge to possess something at all costs. Often a lack of gratitude for what one has received lies at the root of it.

At the Berlin Catholic Convention of 1980, a doctor's wife shared with the audience how she came, in a very personal way, to inner freedom. Her story serves to summarize this chapter.

> The life of a mother is one great adventure. Not a day goes by without surprises. One such adventure that changed my own life and that of our family considerably I want to share with you. I am a mother of five children who are now twenty-one, twenty, nineteen, fifteen, and nine years old. I am a very happy mother now, but that was not always so. There was a time—not so long ago—that I was very unhappy. I realized that I was no longer able to help my children in their problems. We did not understand each other any more. The children withdrew from my husband and me. The situation reached the point that psychological stress affected my health. I experienced heart failure; during the night I could

hardly sleep. The atmosphere in our family was extremely tense.

I prayed much. One day I prayed to the Lord, "Lord, you alone can help. Tell me what I have to do!" And I received the answer, "Give me back your children. I have entrusted them to you for a while so that you can accompany them. But now, give them back into my hand. Don't you think that I can guide them better than you?" And that is what I have done—with much pain and deep joy. Each child individually I gave back to the Lord, with his or her weaknesses and faults, charm and love, hopes and dreams.

How much has changed since then! I am no longer afraid, no matter what happens to my children. If they go along paths which I do not understand, I still am sure: they are held in God's hands. All shall be well.

Something else has changed as well: our family life! Parents and children have found each other anew. Now, during the weekends, our children come home from college not just to get their laundry done, but they look forward with joy to our being together, to our sharing with each other, our experiences and conversations. It seems to me that the Lord has given me back my children in a new way. Thanks be to God!

By your truth, Lord God,
you set free every person
imprisoned in himself or herself.
To freedom you have called us
and to become men and women
in the image and the spirit
of Jesus Christ.
We beseech you,
give us the strength
that his life has first provided,
give us the openness
that he has prepared for us,
make us receptive and free
so that, with you,
we may live for this world, today and every
    day,
forever and ever.

FOUR

"What I do, I do not understand"

The love which God has for us—for each of us as we are—is the content of our faith. We cannot earn God's love; neither can we lose it. It is everlasting. It sets us free. When we are able to truly believe in it, we have nothing to lose and are free people, in the way Jesus lived. To the extent that we believe in this love, we also are able to accept ourselves. There lies the source of genuine freedom. So long as we do not accept ourselves, we cannot be really free, especially in our relationships. That lack of self-acceptance will foster in us the tendency to be selfish, to try to bind others to ourselves, to cling, to take advantage of, and then, of course, to be disappointed time and time again, over and over.

Our freedom also implies—and this is dreadful—that we can either accept God's love or reject it. However, it is rare that we play the game of life with such high stakes. To reject God's love is not something we do easily. Normally we do not play with all or nothing. We prefer to play with small money. We accept and affirm God's love at our baptism, at our confirmation, and at other important moments of our life. In each of us, however, there is also another movement, a motion away from God. Herein lies real danger: that we say "yes" and at the same time take something back; that we let ourselves be drawn toward God, but also keep a cautious distance. After all, God is "a consuming fire" (Heb 12:29); nobody wants to get burned. So there are two movements. The one is toward God, usually in small steps; this movement is strongly emphasized. We dwell on it extensively, we speak and read about it; it is the topic of homilies and conferences. The other one is away from God. This is seldom mentioned, but it is there nonetheless. Insofar as it is ignored, it is all the more insidious. It thrives on compromises, implicit conditions, and half-truths.

That is the way the dynamics of our lives often work: we approach God, and then we retrace our steps—partly. Compromises cripple us. They sap our energy and joy. They corrode like rust which eats away even steel, causing cracks, for instance, in a bridge. In a similar way, our half-hearted "yes" to God weakens the fiber of our lives, though we often notice the effect only after much time has passed. Our compromises and half-measures are so plausible; they seem to make so much sense. We can rationalize them with great conviction. Yet, deep in our heart, we know that something is not right.

In his letter to the Church of Laodicea, the apocalyptic seer of the Book of Revelation writes, "I know your works; I know that you are neither cold nor hot. I wish you were either cold or hot. So, because you are lukewarm, neither hot nor cold, I will spit you out of my mouth" (Rv 3:15-16). One could hardly state more graphically God's intolerance for half-heartedness. Theology and spirituality speak about the mystery of evil, the *mysterium iniquitatis*. This can refer to the terrible mystery whereby we fundamentally refuse our Creator. But perhaps the fact that we can say "yes" to God in the larger context and at the same time "no" in the details is even more awful. It remains so opaque that we do not see through it ourselves, and therefore are inclined to underestimate its evil and to dismiss it with an elegant word like "human condition." With this word we cover up a lot.

Romano Guardini had a long and painful death. When his friend, Walter Dirks, came to visit him, the dying Guardini said, "I am soon going to die and will have to give an account of my life, and I will try to do so to the best of my ability." And then he added, raising his voice slightly, "But I myself also have a question to ask. When I meet God I want to ask him about the mystery of suffering. I do not understand it at all."

Then I say to myself, if Guardini didn't understand it when he was in the midst of it, then we won't be able to understand it either.

There is a mystery to evil. Not only suffering, but especially *guilt* is mysterious. Our guilt is dark and obscure, incomprehensible and inscrutable. In nature there are certain insects which, along with their poisonous venom, also inject anesthetic so that their prey becomes somewhat numb and does not notice clearly what is happening. In sin something similar takes place. Guilt is the silent suffocation of the spirit, if we interpret the spirit as the innermost core of our being, our living relationship with God. All of us accumulate in our lives our own personal guilt, which eventually constitutes a many-linked chain. This chain binds and constricts and stifles our relationships, including our relationship with God.

A Hasidic story points out eloquently the unobtrusive and almost imperceptible root of evil. Rabbi Jizchak Meir said, "When one assumes a position of leadership many things are required: yeshiva, an office, a desk, chairs, an administrator, a janitor, etc. And then comes the evil enemy and takes away the innermost point, but all the rest remains as it was and the wheel keeps turning, only the inner point fails." The rabbi raised his voice, "But God help us; this must not happen!" The inner point is the union with God. It is very possible to have a thriving organization without the inner point. Yet, the inner point is irreplaceable; it alone renders our existence and our activities meaningful. Do we not sometimes endanger that inner point too readily? Are we aware of what is happening there? Guilt usually sneaks in unnoticed, often in the guise of a good intention and common sense. It is in this way that evil persists as a great mystery.

Let us glance quickly at four aspects of this mystery. In the first place, the intellectual aspect. Our intellect feels inadequate in dealing with guilt. That is why Søren Kierkegaard remarks, "No one is capable of recognizing sin by himself. Precisely because we ourselves are in sin, all our speaking about sin is basically a sinful watering down." The essence of sin is untruth, lie, and denial; and therefore it obscures our insight. It is easier than one thinks to fool one's conscience and to adapt oneself to what is not good.

Guilt camouflages its intentions and scope until the false decision has been made and is perhaps even irrevocable. Only when it is too late does its devastating impact reveal itself. That is why the Christian revelation does not begin with our own experience, which is inevitably opaque and largely inaccessible. Rather, it conveys to us the word of God which confronts us. That can sometimes shock us, hopefully in a salutary way. Perhaps we, too, like David, occasionally need such a jolt. The affair of David with Bathsheba (2 Sam 11-12) I find abominable—the adultery of the king with the wife of one of his soldiers in combat. But what happens afterward seems to me even more staggering—how David represses his guilt and uses devious means to trick people into believing that the child to be born was fathered by Uriah. All his power—and the power of a king was considerable—he abuses to deceive. His first move is to have Uriah unexpectedly come home on leave, obviously in the hope that he would be together with his wife. Uriah, however, spends the night in the barracks with the other soldiers, very much to the disappointment of David. The next day David invites Uriah for a grand dinner and makes him drunk. The great psalmist David! After this drinking bout, however, Uriah is clear-headed enough not to go home, but once again he returned to the barracks. The next day David sends Uriah back to the front with this message to Joab, "Place Uriah up front, where the fighting is fierce. Then pull back and leave him to be struck down dead." Incredibly, David does not yet realize that this is a sin, a grievous sin.

Then the prophet Nathan comes to him with a concise, apt parable about a wealthy man who kills the only sheep of a poor peasant to add to his own lavish banquet. David reacts spontaneously and vehemently, "As the Lord lives, the man who has done this merits death!" Enmeshed as he is in the evil he has perpetrated, David still does not understand the point of the parable! *Mysterium iniquitatis.* Nathan needs to accuse him bluntly, "*You* are the man!" Then David recognizes his guilt and is noble enough to admit it. The scales fall from his eyes and he catches sight of his great guilt—yes, it is he.

St. Paul articulated the incomprehensibility of guilt in a classic text: "What I do, I do not understand. For I do not do what I want, but I do what I hate. . . . For I do not do the good I want, but I do the evil I do not want. . . . Miserable one that I am! Who will deliver me from this mortal body?" (Rom 7:15, 19, 24). I don't understand myself at all, Paul sighs.

A second aspect is even more important. Not only can my intellect not understand guilt, but also my heart cannot cope with it. If the heart cannot deal with something, we are easily tempted to repress the thing, that is to say, to hide it away in the subconscious. Then we really do not know it any more and seemingly the problem is gone. That is exactly what David did with his guilt against Uriah: he expelled it from his consciousness. Much to the delight of present day depth psychologists Jesus says, "everyone who does wicked things hates the light and does not come toward the light, so that his works might not be exposed" (Jn 3:20). The evil wants to remain in the darkness. That is its favorite spot. In the dark it can proliferate. That is its world. The evil does not want to surface. I am amazed that this insight is so clearly identified in the psalms, "Who can detect heedless failings? Cleanse me from my unknown faults" (Ps 19:13). Other translations speak about unknown *guilt*. This can indeed happen: guilt of which I am not conscious. At the end of the beautiful Psalm 139, a similar thought is expressed,

"Probe me, God, know my heart;
    try me, know my concerns.
See if my way is crooked,
    then lead me in the ancient paths"
(Ps 139:23-24).

The Old Testament authors apparently knew that a guilty person is inclined to repress his guilt. That is still the case. Much guilt, even grievous guilt, is repressed, denied, concealed, dismissed, or covered up with smart words. The ancient Chinese tried to expel evil spirits with loud noise. That method is still in use! But there are subtler, more cultivated ways to get rid of the burden of our guilt. Whoever is facile with words—commanding an extensive vocabulary—can wrap up what is blameworthy in such a way that it appears innocent and attractive. Someone who is moody or impatient or prejudiced, for example, can hide himself behind his delicate makeup. That sounds good. In religious circles some play this game cleverly.

A third aspect of the mystery of evil is more practical. The evil I commit is always a mixture of impotence and ill will. These two elements are always present, though in varying degrees. There is always an element of weakness in our guilt. No one chooses evil in complete freedom. We don't have to look for the evil, it presents itself. Initially, we resist but after a while we give in. Our weakness gets the upper hand. That element of frailty is always there: we really did not will it, nevertheless we did it. The other element is also always present: our shadow, our malice, the evil in us. After all, I myself choose to do this, it is my own decision. There is always a certain amount of free choice.

Dorothee Soelle relates an experience of a friend who was chaplain at a New York prison. A young man was sentenced to that prison because he had killed his mother. The minister, no doubt with the best of intentions but also with a lack of sensitivity, found all kinds of excuses: "you grew up in Harlem and were exposed to much violence; you experienced far too little love in your youth; life has little or no meaning for you," and so on. At a certain moment the prisoner lost his patience and yelled at him, "Stop it. I *killed* my mother, and that is *bad*!" The minister was bewildered.

What really took place there? A very dangerous scenario. Basically, the minister told the inmate, "You couldn't help it." In this way he robbed the young man of his last bit of self-worth. Fortunately, the prisoner was alert enough to perceive and honest enough to decline the implication of the message being forced on him. This story can teach us the important lesson to take guilt—both our own guilt and the guilt of others—seriously. If we don't, we do not take the person behind that guilt seriously either. To forgive is by no means the same as to gloss over.

The right approach consists in never losing sight of the combination and interplay of two elements: weakness and maliciousness. To isolate the first would mean that we want to, but we cannot. The second by itself alone would say that we can, but we don't really want to. It is vital to understand that the two components are not clearly separated, but merge and interpenetrate. We feel our weakness, but too easily strike a bargain. We experience our inadequacy to live consistently, but also yield prematurely. It is worthwhile to probe, as far as this is possible, the deeper causes of that powerlessness; in the last analysis, we ourselves bear the responsibility for our behavior. How do we deal with these two sides in us? Since we cannot draw a clear boundary between weakness and malevolence, neither can we determine the exact measure of our guilt. Every so often there are people who want to know precisely just how far they are guilty. That can become an obsession. That road, however, leads to a dead end and diverts attention from what is far more important—contrition and forgiveness.

This contains a helpful lesson for our daily life. Our guilt is often connected with the wounds which others have inflicted on us. But how do we deal with these wounds? If we do not deliberately cope with them in a healthy way, we can easily inflict unnecessary pain on others and thus become guilty ourselves. Traumas which have not been integrated can easily trigger untruthfulness, overeating, overdrinking, overdoing, self-abuse, rigidity, unhealthy competition, and pride. These inept and sterile attempts to live with hurts are doomed to failure. And yet, it happens so often. We are victims of some injustice but we may be inclined to obsess over it, to turn it around in our thoughts and words and from that stance react to others. In this way, we in turn hurt others and become guilty ourselves. Often we do not notice that we are caught in a vicious circle which we maintain and even extend. So the victim easily becomes a perpetrator. In such a situation, it is beneficial to quiet oneself, to honestly face one's wounds without giving in to desires of revenge or self-pity, and to seek the door to reconciliation. Only then can something new start.

In this area there are all kinds of underground connections which remain dark and obscure. It helps to know that we touch here the realm of darkness and that we must be on our guard not to get entangled in dismal and disastrous obsessions and fixations. They would block the way to reconciliation. Once again, the truth will set us free.

The fourth aspect is closely connected with the third: we can never fully articulate our guilt. We can only do that partially. Many of us, no doubt, have had that experience ourselves. After a good confession, or after a liberating face-to-face reconciliation, we were very much aware that we had not said everything. That's correct, and very perceptive. We cannot say everything, we cannot express all our guilt. And that is not necessary. Neither God nor the church requires that from us. Counting on the reader's willingness to understand me correctly, I would venture to say that every confession is symbolic. What we confess stands for much more. Maybe an analogy can help. Guilt is like an iceberg. Ninety percent of every iceberg floats under the surface, largely concealed from our eyes. Only ten percent is visible. That is the law of nature pertaining to the specific gravity of ice. Our guilt is like that. The tip of our guilt emerges, is visible, and we are aware of it. Much more, however, is hidden and invisible—the benefit of the subconscious! I would like to stretch this image a little further. There are always people who swim around the iceberg and try to lift it. They should know that this is impossible. What one gains on one side, one loses on the other. It always remains ten percent versus ninety percent. God does not want us to do something so unhealthy, neither does the church require it from us. It is enough to acknowledge and confess what we are aware of without too much of an effort. The center of gravity of the sacrament of reconciliation lies in God's forgiveness, not in our examination of conscience, nor in our confession. There is a real danger in confession becoming deformed or distorted to the point where God is no longer the focus.

When the darkness of our guilt turns out to be so dense and obscure, then a healthy reaction to this mystery of evil is possible only when it comes as a gift—a grace—rather than the result of our own efforts. We cannot make contrition; we receive it. Contrition which we produce ourselves is far too rigid and tense, and sometimes even steeped in a desire to justify ourselves before God. Genuine contrition contains in itself all the fruits of the spirit: peace, confidence, patience, gentleness—yes, even joy (cf. Gal 5:22-23). When these qualities fail in our contrition, then it is too much our own making. We can spare ourselves this trouble. In the third chapter of Lamentations we find,

But I will call this to mind,
as my reason to have hope:
The favors of the LORD are not exhausted,
his mercies are not spent;
They are renewed each morning,
so great is his faithfulness. . . .
Good is the LORD to one who waits for him,
to the soul who seeks him;
It is good to hope in silence
for the saving help of the LORD.

—Lamentations 3:21-23, 25-26

Authentic contrition grows in us when we focus on God rather than ourselves. There can be an awareness of guilt that is too much taken up with self. That is not healthy and not what God desires. In scripture, the awareness of our sins is not meticulously detailed. It finds its source in the encounter with God. After the miraculous catch of fish, Peter said, "Depart from me, Lord, for I am a sinful man" (Lk 5:8). Peter's contrition was not the fruit of a quick examination of conscience, but the reflection of the glory of God which shines in Jesus. Peter then knew intuitively and deeply that he was a sinful man. Isaiah had a similar experience, "Woe is me, I am doomed! . . . my eyes have seen the King, the LORD of hosts!" (Is 6:5).

For a Christian the most appropriate place to come to self-knowledge and contrition is the contemplation of Jesus on the cross. To gaze at Jesus is the fastest and best way to become aware of our guilt, and to open ourselves up to God's merciful love. When we focus on the cross, we cannot gloss over our guilt nor can we say, it was not that bad, really. On the other hand, Jesus on the cross saves us from discouragement and despair. The cross is the worst that the earth did to heaven; at the same time, the cross is the most priceless gift which heaven gave to the earth—love to the very end. Let us focus on this.

Then we shall become aware of our guilt, our repression will be released, and the door will be opened for grace. There, too, we can overcome the temptation that makes us think that God's mercy is not for us, since our guilt is so great. There we get an inkling that we are already forgiven, for "with you is forgiveness and so you are revered" (Ps 130:4).

O God, your name
has been with us on earth
from the beginning,
a word so full of promise
that it has kept us going.
But in Jesus' life and death
you have revealed your name.
You, our Father, can be found
in him for all time.
He is your Word and promise
completely.
We ask you that we may
be drawn to him
and thereby come
to know you more and more,
today and every day
forever and ever.

FIVE

We all need forgiveness

The prophet Micah wonders, "Who is there like you, the God who removes guilt and. . . *delights* . . . in clemency?" (Mi 7:18). God is happy to forgive. We may have our difficulties with the sacrament of reconciliation. Confessing over and over the same sins must be boring for God. Such thinking, however, is a perfect example of projection. In this way we ascribe to God something which *we* find difficult. God knows us far better than we know ourselves, "for God is greater than our hearts and knows everything" (1 Jn 3:20). God understands our particular weaknesses, where we fail so often. God knows that we all have our sins. From our perspective it is very natural that we are often disappointed in ourselves, and eventually might be tempted to think: that is not so bad, that is part of me, it's just the way I am. Some may go as far as to conclude: that's the way God made me. This weakens our sense of guilt and our fervor for progress. It leads to a cheap compromise with our weaknesses and a deliberate choice for mediocrity. Through our faults we can grow, provided we do not settle for them but instead learn to live always on God's forgiveness.

The usual translation of Psalm 130, verse 4, reads, "With you is forgiveness and so you are revered." Another possible translation is, "With you is forgiveness, and *on this we live*."

Forgiveness is healthy food. If it isn't on our menu over a span of time, the health of our spirit is impaired just as surely as our bodies become ill when lacking certain vitamins over a long period.

"Who is there like you, the God . . . who delights in clemency?" There is no need for God to make any great exertion in order to forgive. On the contrary, God delights in forgiving. Forgiveness is the completion of love. In forgiveness love reaches its utmost purity, depth, and strength; and in this way, forgiveness generates new life. This is all the more true for God's love.

The prophet Zephaniah offers us a powerful text. Listen to these words personally, as said to each of us individually:

> Shout for joy, O daughter Zion!
>   sing joyfully, O Israel!
> Be glad and exult with all your heart,
>   O daughter Jerusalem!
> The LORD has removed the judgment against
>   you,
>   he has turned away your enemies;
> The King of Israel, the LORD, is in your midst,
>   you have no further misfortune to fear.
> On that day, it shall be said to Jerusalem:
>   Fear not, O Zion, be not discouraged!
> The LORD, your God, is in your midst,
>   a mighty savior;
> He will rejoice over you with gladness,
>   and renew you in his love,
> He will sing joyfully because of you,
>   as one sings at festivals.
>   —Zephaniah 3:14-17

Let us have the patience and the courage to let these words penetrate, without watering them down, without false self-deprecation, or lack of faith. Let God be God! God delights over us. God rejoices over us and shows it without inhibition. "Who is there like you, the God . . . who delights in clemency?" Please read it yourself and savor it.

Jesus describes this joy of God perhaps even more beautifully and warmly. In Luke's gospel, chapter 15, he tells three parables—the lost sheep, the lost drachma, and the prodigal son. All three make the same point. Three times the parables deal with the joy of the one who finds. First, there is the joy of the shepherd. I suppose that the sheep who was found experienced a great joy, too, but that joy is not mentioned. That is not the point. The message is the joy of the shepherd. "When he does find it, he sets it on his shoulders with great joy and, upon his arrival home, he calls together his friends and neighbors and says to them, 'Rejoice with me because I have found my lost sheep'" (Lk 15:5-6). The second parable speaks to us about the joy of the woman who, after carefully sifting through her dirt floor, finally discovers her lost drachma. "When she does find it, she calls together her friends and neighbors and says to them, 'Rejoice with me because I have found the coin that I lost'" (Lk 15:9). Jesus compares God to a housekeeper who crawls on her knees through the house to search for a lost coin. God is seeking everywhere for the one who is lost. Once again, the theme is the joy of the one who finds!

Finally, Jesus speaks of the joy of the father. No doubt the prodigal son was thrilled with his cordial reception and the unexpectedly great kindness of his father. Yet, this joy of the son is not mentioned at all in the parable; once again, that is not the theme. It is all about the joy of the Father, our God.

A few chapters earlier Jesus was filled with joy and exclaimed, prompted by the Holy Spirit, "I give you praise, Father, Lord of heaven and earth, for although you have hidden these things from the wise and the learned you have revealed them to the childlike. Yes, Father, such has been your gracious will. . . . No one knows who the Son is except the Father, and who the Father is except the Son and anyone to whom the Son wishes to reveal him" (Lk 10:21-22). The latter is exactly what Jesus is doing in this fifteenth chapter: revealing to us who the Father is, giving us a portrait of this Father who rejoices to find us.

The joy of the Father! In this joy, Jesus lives and he longs for us to share in it. "I have told you this so that my joy might be in you and your joy might be complete" (Jn 15:11; cf. 16:24, 17:13). He wants to convey to us an abundance of joy. That happens *par excellence* in our experience of being forgiven. Already the name *Jesus* expresses this, especially in Matthew's explanation. An angel appears to Joseph and tells him, "Joseph, son of David, do not be afraid to take Mary your wife into your home. For it is through the holy Spirit that this child has been conceived in her. She will bear a son and you are to name him Jesus, because he will save his people from their sins" (Mt 1:20-21). Interestingly, Matthew here has moved beyond the etymology. The Aramaic word *Yeshua* means literally "God saves." The words, "from their sins," have been added by Matthew to spell out the mission of Jesus without any ambiguity and thereby to articulate his identity. "He will save his people from their sins." This above all is the joy that Jesus desires to bring us. In this way he wants to reveal to us his Father, and enable us to enter into his relationship with the Father. All who trust him and are led by the Spirit of God are children of God. "For you did not receive a spirit of slavery to fall back into fear, but you received a spirit of adoption, through which we cry, '*Abba*, Father!'" (Rom 8:15). So we are allowed to say "Abba, Father" the way Jesus says it. Ask for the grace to know and love the Father in such a way that we, too, can pray full of confidence and joy "Abba Father," putting aside all arrogance and all hesitance. May we experience in this way the touch of God's mercy and goodness.

The parable of the prodigal son (or more accurately "of the merciful father") is called *evangelium in evangelio*, the gospel within the gospel, the heart of the good news of Jesus. It is so simple that a child understands it and so profound that no person can fully plumb the depths of it. The story begins with the request of the younger son for his share of the inheritance. He is entitled to it, but he wants it prematurely. He cannot wait until his father has died; he wants it right away. He wants now what should be given to him later. He makes his rude and self-serving claim without any respect for the feelings of the one who gives it to him. He demands an autonomy which ignores the existing dependence.

The father respects the free will of his son even though the latter abuses that freedom. The father is a wise man who understands that this departure is inevitable—no force in the world can prevent it. He exerts no pressure, no pressure to stay nor any pressure to return. With that respect he gives his son a most precious gift which will later make a return possible. God never coerces. Here we see the greatness of God's power and the openness of God's love. God surely wants to gain our affection and our dedication, but God always leaves us completely free. Even in the most critical of situations, God respects our freedom.

The parable also describes the consequences of guilt: emptiness and loneliness, no relationships and no communication. As long as the young man had money, he also had many friends. But when the money was gone, his friends disappeared. In his great misery he ends up with the pigs. In this way, Jesus tersely pictures the depth of his wretched state. Pigs are considered in Israel to be unclean animals, and no Jew would ever come in contact with them. Even worse: the pigs have something to eat, and he has nothing to ease his hunger.

Rock bottom, he comes to his senses. He remembers his father and in thinking of him he finds the courage to return home. Granted, his motive is not the most lofty one; it is the hunger and the thought that at his father's place he could get something to eat. Perhaps every return to God is, at some level, a consequence of hunger. "Restless is our heart until it finds rest in you," notes St. Augustine.

When the need is most dire, the son begins to escape from his entanglement, and makes the first step toward liberation, toward true life. "I shall get up and go to my father and I shall say to him, 'Father, I have sinned against heaven and against you'" (Lk 15:18). He speaks clearly in two dimensions: vertical and horizontal. Mature contrition always sees both aspects. He is going to confess to his father, "I have sinned. . . ."

Articulating one's guilt is a sign of true contrition. By contrast, preoccupation with guilt that revolves around itself without ever speaking up becomes debilitating, depressing. Such unhealthy awareness of guilt stays trapped in a monologue, in a vicious circle. Authentic awareness of guilt, on the other hand, leads to dialogue, to explicit confession. Expression of one's guilt is a profound human need. The prodigal son is going to add, "I no longer deserve to be called your son; treat me as you would treat one of your hired workers" (Lk 15:19). In true contrition we readily give up our pretensions, relying on a new conviction: "With you is forgiveness and on this we live."

Whoever has experienced contrition and forgiveness in this way comes to a new way of life. He is changed. His stance in the community is different. Whoever has experienced reconciliation is freed from worry about his own image and prestige, from the fear of losing face. Forgiveness liberates and enriches our life. We then know ourselves held with our strengths and weaknesses, with our good and evil, by God who has already reconciled to himself (see 2Cor 5:18). There is no longer a need for us to make the other person small in order to build ourselves up, to put the other person in the shadow, but we can let others shine and rejoice in that. There is no longer a need to be always right and always the best— rather, others are welcome to that privilege, too. Concern for our own advantage gives way to rejoicing in the successes of others. This life style becomes possible when we live on forgiveness.

The son courageously carries out his resolution, breaking away from his misery: so he got up and went back to his father. Now we come to the climax of the parable. "While he was still a long way off, his father caught sight of him, and was filled with compassion. He ran to his son, embraced him and kissed him" (Lk 15:20). No senior in Palestine would ever go toward a junior. No patriarch would ever be the first to rise. He would wait, sitting, and receive the other's homage. But the father in this parable is different from other fathers. He does not ask himself, What am I going to do? Shall I let him in or send him back? What conditions shall I set? No, the overriding emotion of the father is one of overwhelming mercy and intense joy. "Who is there like you, the God . . . who delights in clemency?"

That is the first thing that hits the son, the tremendous joy of his father. It is also the last thing he had expected. I imagine that the son on his way home had played in his mind all kinds of scenarios: how his father could possibly react to his return, and how he would respond to that reaction. But *this* possibility did not cross his mind. His imagination did not go so far that he could see his father running toward him and hugging him full of joy. The joy of the father! Here we find the heart of this parable. This immense joy is a sign and an expression of the father's love. The father would not have been so happy if he had written off his son.

A little sentence of Werner Bergengruen leads us more deeply into this parable. "Love proves its authenticity in fidelity, but reaches its completion in forgiveness." This profound truth applies not only to human love, but also to God's love. God's love proves its authenticity in fidelity and finds its completion in forgiveness. Since the essence of God *is* love, we can say that God's being finds its completion, so to speak, in forgiveness. In this way we can somehow understand why God finds such excessive joy in mercy. God is most divine in forgiving. God is most God when forgiving; this is the secret of God's joy. To be able to experience something of this divine joy is for each of us a great grace. In the Canticle of Zechariah, we pray, "You will give God's people 'knowledge of salvation through the forgiveness of their sins, because of the tender mercy of our God by which the daybreak from on high will visit us'" (Lk 1:77-78).

The knowledge of salvation, the tender mercy of our God, the daybreak from on high—all this happens in the forgiveness of sins. This is what Zechariah announced, what Werner Bergengruen summarized, and what the prodigal son experienced.

God's love, we have seen in Chapter two, is based on nothing. In forgiveness we can experience this truth. We come, not only with empty hands—if only they were empty!—but with hands full of the broken pieces of our lives. And yet, we are welcomed with a grand reception and enormous joy, with the finest robe, with shoes and a ring, with a festive dinner and music. In this way, we can really experience that God's love is based on nothing, and sets no conditions. Thus, we come to the foundation of our life. In the sacrament of reconciliation we can experience in the depth of our heart that even in our guilt, at our worst, we are fully accepted and heartily welcomed. That gives us an inkling of the immensity of the father's love. The father encompasses his son with his love as with a festive robe. The vocabulary of the father speaks of joy and feast, my son and my child, found and come to life again. The vocabulary of the son describes hunger and need, pigs and loneliness, hired worker and undeserving servant. Forgiveness literally transfers the son into the world of his father. God "delivered us from the power of darkness and transferred us to the kingdom of his beloved Son, in whom we have redemption, the forgiveness of sins" (Col 1:13-14).

Reconciliation always has global and even cosmic ramifications. In our personal reconciliations, peace takes hold in our small world, a peace which then expands to reconcile and heal well beyond the confines of our own hearts. At the same time, some reconciliation and reparation of the larger world occurs. It begins when, in our own hearts, a little bit more of the kingdom of God comes through to our troubled world. It ripples out in ever-widening circles of forgiveness, reconciliation, and love.

All of us, especially those more advanced in years, learned well to prepare ourselves for the sacrament of reconciliation. But most of us give little thought to what comes after confession. It's truly an underdeveloped area in our tradition. Of course, we complete our penance and perhaps we even take time for a short prayer of thanksgiving, but that is usually the extent of it. This is a great pity, because what comes *after* confession is no less important than what comes before it. Certainly it requires no less time. To accept and absorb forgiveness is a process that needs time and should not be broken off prematurely. This process is only completed when we have forgiven ourselves and are truly at peace.

After confession, there is a double joy. First, there is a joy of relief that we have confessed. Then there is a second joy: the joy with which God forgives and into which God literally invites us. The joy of our God! The great surprise of the prodigal son was the joy of his father. In no way had he expected it. The joy of his father has deeply touched and gladdened him. The grace we are talking about here is to experience and savor something of this joy of the father. Of course, we cannot produce this joy, but we can open ourselves for it and pray for this grace. This joy is very important, because only in joy does new life blossom and grow. Willpower and resolutions by themselves cannot achieve fruit that endures. But what comes forth from joy has a future.

God does not gloss over our guilt; neither does God condone our sin. On the contrary, God takes our guilt very seriously, deadly seriously. God does not do away with our guilt with a small gesture. The ever-faithful God of the covenant absorbs the suffering of those who are unfaithful. This rupture of the covenant leads God into the passion of love, the passion of the cross. "For the love of Christ impels us, once we have come to the conviction that one died for all; therefore, all have died. He indeed died for all, so that those who live might no longer live for themselves but for him who for their sake died and was raised" (2 Cor 5:14-15). In St. Paul's message, the biblical idea and the profound reality of representation play a vital role. At the end of this passage he writes, "For our sake [God] made him to be sin who did not know sin, so that we might become the righteousness of God in him" (2 Cor 5:21). The sins of humankind spent all their malice and energy in the death of Jesus, and thus lost their sting. The way to reconciliation is now open.

The English Benedictine Sebastian Moore captures this reconciliation in a profound image. Evil, he writes, is present in a diffused way everywhere in our world, also in ourselves, in me, like a very fine dust, like a gas that permeates everything. It is present in all that we do, but impossible to grasp, like a kind of ether. When, however, the All Holy enters this world, evil suddenly crystallizes. The evil that had always been so elusive, becomes massive and dense. It makes a fist and nails the All Holy to the cross. It releases all its anger on the person of Jesus, unto his death. The death of Jesus is not some kind of cruel ransom paid to the Father. Rather, in the death of Jesus, evil has expended all its energy and thereby lost its potency.

Lord God, ─────────
anyone who has finally settled with you
can always go back to you—
there is nothing that cannot be restored with
    you.
Only your love will not be revoked.
We pray, God,
remind us of your name
so that we may turn again to you,
be our father and our mother
again and again
and give us life,
as a happiness we do not deserve,
today and every day
forever and ever.

Six

"I have chosen you to go out and to bear fruit"

The crowning of forgiveness is undoubtedly that the person forgiven receives once more the full confidence of the one forgiving and is entrusted again with a mission. Perhaps we can interpret the word "re-mission" this way. Mission is always a matter of trust. In the Hebrew language there is a word *shaliach* which means a person who is sent. Mission plays an important and very lovely role in the Jewish culture, and therefore also in scripture.

Chapter twenty-four of the book of Genesis relates how Abraham "in his ripe old age" sends his senior servant Eliezer to Haran in order to find a wife for his only son, Isaac. It is a magnificent chapter. The dignified behavior of Eliezer is anything but slavish. He chooses from his master's possessions ten camels, all kinds of silver and golden presents and fine clothing. He needs these for his mission. Then he sets out for Haran where his master, Abraham still has relatives. There, too, his behavior is courtly and noble, and at the same time full of respect for his master. He never loses sight of the intention of Abraham. When dinner is ready, he does not go to the table until he has explained the message of his master, because he knows that Abraham would do likewise. He graciously combines great conviction and vigor with a clear harmony with the intentions of his master. Not even in his dreams can any thought surface that would sway him from his mission. Mission is a matter of trust, and that trust he will not break. He comes as an emissary of Abraham; this shapes his whole demeanor.

Eliezer comes to look for a wife for his master's only son. This is a good example of a mission in everyday life. Jewish culture is replete with them. Of course, specifically religious missions also abound. The rabbis use a maxim which says, "A *shaliach* is like the person who sends him," like an alter ego. The essence of the mission is the relationship of trust between the one who sends and the one who is sent. These two persons must be in harmony. It is not important whether the mission implies a long or a short trip, or perhaps no trip at all. Mission can very well take place in *stabilitas loci*, the stability to their abbey to which Benedictines bind themselves. In present day English, *mission* often has the connotation of an impressive achievement which enables one to say at the end proudly, "mission accomplished." That is not necessarily an element of the biblical concept of mission; it need not be something great. Far more important is the trust which the master grants his *shaliach* and which the latter seeks to honor at all costs.

We could describe mission as representation. The *shaliach* re-presents his or her master. If we take the word *representation* in its most literal, rich meaning, it might be the best definition of mission. The *shaliach* renders the master present and active. In the *shaliach* the master speaks and operates. What the *shaliach* agrees upon, promises, or signs, binds the master not only morally, but also legally. The master gives his *shaliach*, so to speak, a blank check, and binds himself in advance to the decisions the *shaliach* will make. So much trust is included in the mission.

This presupposes on the part of the *shaliach* an indispensable unselfishness. It would be absurd to send a selfish person on a mission. Only self-forgetful persons can represent their master. In the *shaliach* there must be room for the person who sends her. Perhaps it is even more accurate to say, whoever accepts a mission needs to be transparent. The master should shine through her. This requires a great clarity so that the master is seen through the emissary.

The older I become, the more important transparency has become for me. Words can sometimes be rather cheap. The motives for our deeds can be mixed, unknown even to ourselves. Transparency, however, is unambiguous. The light shines through. This is what we need.

Jesus was a completely transparent person. "Whoever has seen me has seen the Father." (Jn 14:9). The Father shone through him. To put oneself forward is the exact opposite of mission and transparency. Egoism muddles, darkens, and ultimately destroys credibility. In scripture we find many instances of the so-called *shaliach* principle, which Jesus uses regularly: "Amen, amen, I say to you, whoever receives the one I send receives me, and whoever receives me receives the one who sent me" (Jn 13:20). We find this principle also in its negative form, "Whoever rejects you rejects me. And whoever rejects me rejects the one who sent me" (Lk 10:16). Still another example, where Jesus cried out, "Whoever believes in me believes not only in me but also in the one who sent me, and whoever sees me sees the one who sent me" (Jn 12:44-45).

In his baptism Jesus very consciously took upon himself his mission. It was a loaded moment, and an intimate event, that took place between the Father and the Son in the Holy Spirit (in the form of a dove, as scripture says). John the Baptist witnessed the baptism and heard the voice of the Father. In his baptism Jesus gave himself completely to the Father and offered himself fully to the mission which the Father entrusted to him. He was very much aware that his whole life was at stake, that he had been anointed to bring glad tidings to the poor and sent to proclaim liberty to captives (cf. Lk 4:18). This was to consume his whole person—indeed his whole life. His public life, his passion, and his death are consequences of this baptism. It is all implied. Jesus had needed thirty years of hidden life to prepare himself for this baptism, for the acceptance of his mission; the three remaining years he needed to realize his baptism. He did so with utmost dedication and fidelity.

What enabled this fidelity? Listen to John's gospel in which Jesus says, "My food is to do the will of the one who sent me and to finish his work" (Jn 4:34). The loving will of his Father shapes his life, is the content of his life, is the food on which he feeds. "I came down from heaven not to do my own will but the will of the one who sent me" (Jn 6:38). He is completely transparent. "The one who sent me is with me. He has not left me alone, because I always do what is pleasing to him" (Jn 8:29). Mission resides in union with God and union with God exists only in mission: surrendering to God from the morning to the evening and then throughout the night. In such loving abandon Jesus lived his union with the Father. Likewise for us. When we know ourselves as *sent* and we live on that mission, we are one with the God-who-sends. Apart from union with God, mission is not possible, just as apart from the mission, union with God is impossible.

The roots of Jesus' mission go deep. They reach into the unfathomable mystery of the Trinity. There, the source of all love and of all life, we find also the origin of all mission. From all eternity the Son has come forth from the Father, and the Father has given God's own fullness wholly to the Son. The mystery of Trinity implies giving life in unending self-emptying. The Father gives completely to the Son without keeping anything back—the Son surrenders completely to the Father without any reserve. That is what lovers do: they give themselves completely in order to beget life. How could it be otherwise for God-who-is-love?

When the fullness of time had come, the procession of the Son from the Father was continued in the mission of the Son into the world. This mission stands also in the context of *kenosis*:

> he emptied himself,
> taking the form of a slave,
> coming in human likeness;
> and found human in appearance,
> he humbled himself,
> becoming obedient to death,
>> even death on a cross (Phil 2:7-8).

When the earthly life of Jesus came to an end, Jesus spoke twice the same sentence, once in the form of a prayer (Jn 17:18) and once addressing the disciples: "As the Father has sent me, so I send you" (Jn 20:21). The mission, from and for which he lived and which formed the content of his life, he passed on to his disciples. We have to continue his mission. From now on Jesus has no other hands, no other mouth, and no other heart than ours. St. Paul captures its essence simply in these words, "I live, no longer I, but Christ lives in me" (Gal 2:20).

There we find both the meaning and the eternal destiny of our lives: "Those he foreknew [God] also predestined to be conformed to the image of his Son, so that he might be the first-born among many brothers [and sisters]" (Rom 8:29). Conforming our lives to the image of God's Son means becoming sons and daughters of God as Jesus was. It also entails accepting his lifestyle, living as he did. That mission requires from us an intimate union with Jesus just as he was intimately united with the Father. Jesus expressed this marvelously in the parable of the vine and the branches. He is the vine, we are the branches. It is obvious that a branch not connected with the vine cannot bear any fruit. It is dead wood. Only the sap of the vine can make the branch fruitful. It is the life of Jesus that bears fruit in us (Jn 15:1-8).

We are invited to accept our mission anew every day. I am convinced that a mission which is set once and for all is an inner contradiction. Mission means living with open hands. An elderly man once shared with me confidentially that he began each day by prostrating himself for ten minutes with the palms of his hands open. In doing so he gave his whole day to the Lord and accepted everything that God would send him. What impressed me very much in this man was how flexible he remained in his old age, and how easily he could adapt to the unforeseen. I assume that the secret of his availability lies in the first ten minutes of his day.

Mission creates a vital tension in our lives. There are, of course, unhealthy tensions which are harmful for the life between spouses, in a family, in a religious community, in a workplace, or in our personal life. But there are also vital tensions which promote and enrich life, which keep us fit and supple. Mission creates such a lively tension. On the one hand, we are wholly present wherever we are, not flitting about and not daydreaming but focused with genuine dedication of heart and soul to our task. On the other hand, we remain available to be missioned elsewhere or in another way at any time. Therefore, it is good to take up our mission fresh each morning, as if it were completely new. Perhaps for many years it is the same each time, but there may come a day when a different mission presents itself. Whoever remains willing to accept that change is attentively living her mission. Whoever has completely identified himself or herself with a particular task or place cannot change any more and will be devastated when another mission comes. The change may make such a person suspicious. What did I do wrong? What are they "cooking up" for me? Why this shift? The vital tension has been lost.

All who genuinely live their mission experience an inner freedom. Mission makes us free. Whoever lacks a sense of mission is easily tempted to carry the burden too much alone. Someone has called this syndrome The God Complex: to rely too little on God while acting as if one were God. In our mission we are carried by God and the ultimate responsibility rests with God.

Unless our sense of mission remains alive and keeps on growing, we risk its diminishment in our lives, and perhaps even its demise. Mission requires tending. We "prepare the way" for the deepening of mission in three crucial ways:

- We select and safeguard quality time for prayer. We decide that God comes before all else and structure our days accordingly. We bring a deliberate quality of attentiveness to times reserved for prayer. We acknowledge that this relationship matters more than any other.

- We pay attention to our ongoing human development. We learn about ourselves, taking steps to integrate our shadow side, seeking direction and counsel, befriending others, taking seriously the call to become whole.

- We choose a discipline that leads us more and more toward basic integrity. We find balance with regard to food and drink, exercise, and sleep. We keep watch over what we say and do, how authentically and honestly we live. We prefer transparency rather than always trying to "look good" in the sight of others.[1]

It is striking that in John's Gospel, Jesus says two sentences which are almost identical: the one reads, "As the Father has sent me, so I send you" (Jn 20:21) and the other, "As the Father loves me, so I also love you" (Jn 15:9). Mission and love are obviously connected, even inter-changeable. Mission is the concrete shape of love. Think of mission as the riverbed of love. A river needs a bed; without a bed it sinks into a swamp. Undoubtedly, the riverbed constrains the water's flow; the path of the stream is set by it. On the other hand, the riverbed gives depth and power to the stream. Without the bed the river stops being a river. In a similar way mission is the riverbed of our love. Of course, mission curtails our love and we sometimes experience the pain of that. Then we would vehemently like to widen the bed, to get out of it. And yet, without the bed our love would silt up and turn into a morass. The mission, though not always easy, is a blessing that makes our love authentic and strong, profound and fruitful.

"Mission is resting in the movement of God."[2] God is motion, energy, the tremendous dynamic of love. From this dynamic stems the whole of creation—so dynamic is our God. At the same time, God is also rest, because God does not strive for a goal. God does not want to achieve anything. This is the dynamic of love. Mission, though active, means at the same time resting in this God-flow. We surrender ourselves to this divine movement, we let ourselves be carried buoyantly by the dynamic of God, like floating on the waves of an immense sea of love. Then we live in harmony with the deepest desires of our own heart, with the ground of our being. That is union with God.

The Bishop of Aachen, Heinrich Mussinghoff, once began his Lenten pastoral with a striking analogy. "The Jordan River originates at the foothills of the snow-capped Hermon, flows through the Sea of Galilee and ends in the Dead Sea. The Sea of Galilee teems with life. It takes in the fresh water and passes it on. Fish thrive in it, olive trees and palms and all kinds of flowers and plants flourish on its banks. Birds and animals find plentiful food there. The Dead Sea, however, is completely different. The Jordan flows into it but finds no outlet. The hot sun evaporates its waters, increasing the salinity to the point where nothing survives. On its shores there are hardly any trees or shrubs. All one sees is salt and desert." The same water! Where it can flow freely, fruitfulness abounds; where it cannot flow, the sea creates a salted wasteland, without fruit and without life. Love needs a bed in order to continue its movement. Only then is life fruitful and worthwhile. Jesus says, "It was not you who chose me, but I who chose you and appointed you to go and bear fruit that will remain" (Jn 15:16). We all know the only thing that really remains and counts is love. Even faith and hope come to an end, but love lasts. Love is the content of our mission: to let ourselves be loved, to love in turn, and to pass on this love to others.

Mission is lived from a fullness, not from an emptiness. A marriage or a religious profession, family or community life, a ministry or a project—if we do not live out of a fullness, these lead to nothing. Mission, however, is possible when we find a plenitude like the man who found a treasure in a field and, full of joy, sold everything he had to obtain it (Mt 13:44). Because he found this precious treasure, he could joyfully give up everything else he had possessed. That is how it is with the kingdom of God, Jesus says. That is what it means to live in gospel fullness.

Living in such fullness, we can give and let go. Then, no matter what our circumstances in life, we can concern ourselves entirely with following Jesus and experience a deep peace in it. But if we try to follow Jesus only because we feel empty and frustrated, if we look for community only because we feel lonely or for ministry in order to find affirmation, we will not succeed. This can easily turn into a half-hearted life. This is not resting in the motion of God. This is not a life resting in the center, but roaming at the fringes. The big question that dominates such a life will be: can I or can I not combine this with my marriage, my vows, or my commitment? Is this within the boundaries or outside? Such a way of life makes us discontent. The gospel does not teach us to live this way. The gospel proclaims authentic joy. In marriage, in religious life, as a single person, as someone searching—we are all invited to live in the center point of fullness where God dwells.

E ternal God,
we bear your name, your imprint.
You have impressed your Son,
your likeness, on us
and we are yours.
We ask you
that we may be like him,
that we may mirror your existence
and reflect your grace
in all our human contacts,
as Christ our brother did
in serving this world
today and every day,
forever and ever.

SEVEN

"I have given you an example"

In John's gospel we read, "during supper, fully aware that the Father had put everything into his power and that he had come from God and was returning to God, [Jesus] rose . . ." (Jn 13:2-4). This verse wonderfully articulates the sense of mission which inspired Jesus. The Father had put everything into Jesus' power—he is the *shaliach* who has come from God and is returning to God. Just as he commissioned us, so his own mission must also bear fruits that remain, fruits of love. Precisely this, he is going to do now to its ultimate outcome. "Jesus loved his own in the world and now he loved them to the end." We could say that, in the Last Supper and what this entails, the mission of Jesus reaches its completion. We can draw from its fullness in eucharist

The first three gospels—the synoptic gospels—and St. Paul give descriptions of the Last Supper which parallel one another. John, however, gives a completely different account. Scripture thus provides us with two views on the same event. With two eyes, one sees depth and perspective, which is not possible using only one eye. We can pray for the grace that these two approaches reveal to us something of the depth of this mystery.

Let us begin with Luke's gospel.

> When the day of the feast of Unleavened Bread arrived, the day for sacrificing the Passover lamb, [Jesus] sent out Peter and John, instructing them, "Go and make preparations for us to eat the Passover." They asked him, "Where do you want us to make the preparations?" And he answered them, "When you go into the city, a man will meet you carrying a jar of water. Follow him into the house that he enters and say to the master of the house, 'The teacher says to you, "Where is the guest room where I may eat the Passover with my disciples?"' He will show you a large upper room that is furnished. Make the preparations there." Then they went off and found everything exactly as he had told them, and there they prepared the Passover.
>
> —Luke 22:7-13

A strange beginning. Luke's intent is not to describe Jesus as a fortune-teller; rather he wants to bring out the sovereign attitude of Jesus in his passion. Passion and death are not a fate that falls upon Jesus. The mystery of the emptying of self is not forced upon him. Jesus is prepared; or rather, he is preparing himself. In the passage which we just quoted, the word "preparation" occurs four times. Jesus approaches the last evening of his life consciously and deliberately. "He said to them, 'I have eagerly desired to eat this Passover with you before I suffer'" (Lk 22:15). Jesus willingly enters into it. A little later he will say, "This is my body, which will be given for you" (Lk 22:19). If Jesus had not given himself, his passion would not have been fruitful. One can apply here the profound thought of Carl Gustav Jung, "We can change only that which we have accepted." Jesus accepted his passion and in so doing transformed it. If he had not embraced it, if he had not given himself, then he would have died a disappointed and bitter person. It is essential for the celebration of the eucharist that Jesus was ready to give himself.

Self-emptying is the shape of divine love. The Trinity is the mystery of self- emptying. Selfish love seeks itself, is possessive and clinging, on the level of material things and even more in the realm of feelings, affirmation, and power. Selfishness and desire to dominate are heavy opponents of love, no matter what the setting: in the family, in marriage, in religious life, in the single state, and everywhere else. Authentic love gives itself as Jesus did. He emptied himself into an unfair trial, a cruel passion, and a shameful death.

To descend is a key theme in the life of Jesus. Jesus, "though he was in the form of God, did not regard equality with God something to be grasped. Rather, he emptied himself . . . " (Phil 2:6-7). He descended with Mary and Joseph to Nazareth and was obedient to them. He went down into the Jordan and took the sins of the people on himself. He went down and became obedient to death, even death on the cross.

"This is my body . . . this is my blood. . . ." The eucharist is the sign and the shape of extreme self-emptying: a piece of bread and a sip of wine—one cannot go any further. The eucharist is completely in line with the life of Jesus. It is not a problem at all, but it is a great mystery. Problems we must solve as far as we can. Mysteries we cannot and must not solve, because then something very precious would get lost. We dwell in mysteries. They provide us a home. They give us security and something to hold onto. It is a poor person who has no mysteries; he is indeed homeless. The eucharist is a profound mystery. We can live in it. Out of this mystery, we can extend the mission of Jesus. Eucharist is typical for Jesus. It is a full-length portrait. Let it be our guide and inspiration.

In the synoptic accounts of the Last Supper, Luke describes something shocking which the others do not mention: "Then an argument broke out among them [the disciples] about which of them should be regarded as the greatest"

(Lk 22:24). A dispute erupted! So completely contrary to the eucharist. How much Jesus must have suffered at that last meal which he had desired so eagerly, when he discovered that his disciples had understood nothing of his spirit and his mentality. His farewell dinner was ruined. The meaning of his life had been missed by his closest friends. The disciples made it abundantly clear to him that they had ideals quite different from his own. They are poles apart from what Jesus is all about. "Then an argument broke out among them about which of them should be regarded as the greatest."

Imagine a feast which one has been anticipating with great expectation. But then, it turns out that none of the guests understand the meaning of it. Such a feast becomes very lonely and disappointing. Luke 22:24 contains an important hint. Let us be honest. Many arguments, though they may appear to be about other things, are basically about the question of which of us is the greatest. "I have more experience. I am more informed. I have more education. I have more insight. I know better." And many more variations on the same theme. But in the last analysis, what we can try to drive home is that we are greater than the other. Such a stance does not fit with the eucharist. It goes against it. From a position of dominance we cannot celebrate eucharist.

We learned in catechesis and theology that eucharist is a sacrament, even the greatest of the seven, and that the sacraments work *ex opere operato*, which means independent of the holiness (or lack thereof) of the person who ministers the sacrament. That is true. But the *reception* of the sacrament does depend on us. The effects of the sacrament are affected by the manner in which they are received. With much pain and confusion, each of us individually and also all of us together as community must learn that rituals, symbols, and even sacraments can become empty; they retain their vitality only if our inner disposition is in agreement. If not, they die out, and even worse: they can become lethal. There is a connection here with the lack of basic integrity. Each of us celebrates eucharist in a fruitful way when we try to live the eucharist in all sincerity. In our brokenness, of course, we will never be perfect, but when we are open to God, sincere in our desire for wholeness, then God continues to hold us, even in our weak moments.

Jesus handed us something infinitely precious—namely, himself in his complete self-surrender. This calls for the greatest respect and love on our part. Of course we all experience distractions at times during the liturgy; that is almost unavoidable. But beneath those distractions we must deal with something far more serious: Is my way of living in harmony with the eucharist? Do I celebrate eucharist while being (before, after, and maybe even during it) involved in an argument—in my heart only, or also in my exterior behavior—about which of us is the greatest? One or the other must die out: that argument or the eucharist.

With three increasingly clear strikes of a gong, the Last Supper is announced as the central, decisive event. First Luke says, "Now the feast of Unleavened Bread, called the Passover, was drawing near" (Lk 22:1). Then, "When the day of the feast of Unleavened Bread arrived . . ." (Lk 22:7). And finally, "When the hour came, [Jesus] took his place at table with the apostles" (Lk 22:14). The feast, the day, the hour—now the great hour in the life of Jesus arrives, the hour about which he had spoken so often.

The main dish of that meal was a one-year old lamb of which no bone was to be broken. The Old Testament gives meticulous directives for the Passover meal, which clarify for us the course of events of the Last Supper. It says the lamb "shall not be eaten raw or boiled, but roasted whole, with its head and shanks and inner organs. . . . You shall not break any of its bones" (Ex 12:9, 46). That lamb, in its entirety, was on the table and could not be overlooked. Peter and John were sent ahead to roast the lamb. When the disciples saw the lamb on the table, they were reminded of the past, of the Exodus from Egypt, and all the wonders that accompanied it. When Jesus saw the lamb, he also looked forward to the future, that is, the immediate future which would begin this very evening. When Jesus saw the lamb, he knew with deep conviction that from this point forward he, himself, would be the "lamb led to the slaughter" (Is 53:7), as expressed in the fourth "Song of the Servant of the Lord," or as "the trusting lamb" prophesied by Jeremiah (Jer 11:19). Now the hour has come to fulfill the prophetic words of John the Baptist: "Behold, the Lamb of God, who takes away the sin of the world" (Jn 1:29).

St. Paul writes, "As often as you eat this bread and drink the cup, you proclaim the death of the Lord until he comes" (1 Cor 11:26). This word applies to every eucharistic celebration. When Jesus broke the bread, he said explicitly, "This is my body." So he breaks his own body. That is where the passion begins, and also the mystical body which is the church. Jesus was fully aware of what he was doing. Perhaps his hands trembled a little when he broke the bread. Let us, too, try to be aware what we do when we celebrate eucharist. Let us continue to proclaim the death of the Lord until he comes.

Our liturgy should not only remember the past, but also look to the future. Eucharist recalls Jesus who died, faithfully fulfilling his mission; and affirms that this same Jesus rose and will come again. We proclaim it solemnly at the center of eucharist, "When we eat this bread and drink this cup we proclaim your death, Lord Jesus, until you come in glory." The eucharistic meal points toward the heavenly meal. Just as the life of Jesus finds its completion in the eucharist, so the eucharist finds its completion in the eternal banquet.

Jesus was sent to establish the new covenant. The eucharist is the living testament to this: the everlasting presence of Jesus among us. "This cup is the new covenant in my blood, which will be shed for you." The core of the Old Testament was always, "I am your God and you are my people." This covenant has been renewed many times in an ever-greater intimacy, eventually even compared with the intimacy of marriage. God and his people are bound together like bridegroom and bride. The new covenant is its fulfillment in a still greater intimacy, "Whoever eats my flesh and drinks my blood remains in me and I in him" (Jn 6:56).

Now let us contemplate how the fourth gospel presents the Last Supper. Immediately in the first verse John offers us the key which gives us access to the mystery of the eucharist: Jesus "loved his own in the world and he loved them to the end" (Jn 13:1). It is all about Jesus' love to the very end. Jesus was always the man for others; now he goes in his mission to the extreme, and gives himself completely for all of us. John does not mention the words of the consecration; instead, he describes the washing of the feet. Apparently, for John, the washing of the feet is just as characteristic and essential for the eucharist as the words of the consecration are for the synoptics. These are the two perspectives which together show us something of the depth of this mystery of love.

Then John writes, "fully aware that the Father had put everything into his power and that he had come from God and was returning to God, he rose from supper and took off his outer garments" (Jn 13:3-4). The washing of the feet begins with Jesus making himself very small. He did so in the fullness of his self-awareness. He knew very well that the Father had put everything into his hands, and that he had come from God and was returning to God. Precisely this awareness enabled him to humble himself so deeply. It is important to remember this when we later hear Jesus' appeal to follow his example. We make ourselves small when we have a strong sense of our self worth, loved by a faithful God. When we forget that it is harder to take the lower place freely, and if we are forced to do so, it creates interior havoc. Genuine humility presupposes an honest self-acceptance. Insofar as our self-acceptance is weak, our freedom to make ourselves small is limited. Our self-acceptance is grounded in the ever-constant love of God for us.

Perhaps the best way to approach this topic is this: Jesus did not dodge confrontation. Jesus bore with many conflicts. In this he was free and courageous. I also believe that afterwards he slept well. He really could cope with conflicts. That is not everyone's gift. When a conflict arises, some people very soon become spiteful and unfair. Jesus never did. He was sovereign—clear and unswerving—in resolving conflicts. He was also sovereign enough to wash the feet of his disciples and to bow down that much. So we notice these two very different qualities in the person of Jesus, both rooted in the same fullness of his self-awareness. Jesus knows how to reach his goal despite the resistance of others; and Jesus can yield and make himself small. The risk of putting this in a general way consists in this: that the ambitious pick up that they should not yield in conflicts, but fight back; and that the meek ones learn that they have to bow, to kneel, to wash another's feet. In this way, each of them misses precisely the appeal meant for him or her. What we need here is discernment of spirits. Words alone are not sufficient, not even the words of sacred scripture. We need the Holy Spirit, who enlightens and guides us and who teaches us to understand the word of God in such a way that we come closer to God. The evil spirit, cunning and experienced, uses even scripture for his own purposes; our shadow will interpret the message the wrong way. Nothing can replace the Holy Spirit. It was precisely in this Spirit that Jesus emptied himself and washed the feet of his disciples.

The apostles, Peter in the first place, are bewildered and disturbed. They do not know how to react. What Jesus is going to do does not fit their worldview at all. Peter in dismay asked, "Master, are *you* going to wash *my* feet?" Jesus insists, "What I am doing, you do not understand now, but you will understand later." Peter stiffens his resistance, "You will never wash my feet." But Jesus, too, holds his ground, "Unless I wash you, you will have no inheritance with me." It is not easy to accept the love of Jesus, neither in its lofty forms nor in its emptying itself. It is not easy to let oneself be loved by Jesus completely. Something in us rebels against it. But Jesus says, "If you do not allow my love to the very end, you do not belong to me."

Let us contemplate with profound respect how Jesus washed the feet of his disciples. First of all, the feet of Peter who complied because he wanted to belong to Jesus. That is by far his highest priority. Then Jesus comes to the sons of thunder, John and James, who had urged Jesus to burn down a whole village because they were not well received. These are the same two careerists who behind the back of the others had requested the first places in the kingdom to come. Jesus at that time had answered, "You do not know what you are asking." Now they get an inkling of what the kingdom of God is all about—foot-washing and self-emptying!

We see how Jesus comes to Matthew to render him the slave's service. Matthew had been a rich man, possessing slaves who had often washed his feet. But now the Master is doing this to him, and it is a very unsettling experience.

Jesus also comes to Judas. Yes, Jesus washed Judas's feet! That is appalling. What went on in the heart of Judas? In the heart of Jesus? The love of Jesus is utterly inclusive. He excluded no one, not even the person who had in mind to betray him that very night, turning him over to his enemies.

Jesus is the image of the Father. "Whoever sees me, sees the Father." From Jesus we can learn how God is. God as the host who receives, God as the one who has room for everyone, not just for people of an ideal world in which sin does not occur, but for each person of our messy world which is sometimes so full of treason and spite. Such is the hospitality of our God, such is God's love to the very end. It shows itself in a context of betrayal, enmity, and rejection. In this broken world Jesus lived and loved. Such a love could not but end on the cross.

Then *my* turn comes. Jesus asks me whether he may wash my feet. I am aware that if I accept, I am going to share in his joy and his passion, in his victory and his conflict, in his life and in his death. Am I ready? Am I ready to wear his garments? Am I ready to live in his spirit? Am I ready to love as he loves? That, too, pertains to the authenticity of the eucharist.

In the synoptics Jesus says, "Do this in memory of me." In John, he says, "You should do as I have done for you." Only in this way can we genuinely celebrate eucharist: if we try to follow him, to do as he did. Then we, too, have to wash the feet of others, yes, even of "our Judas." "You should do as I have done for you."

Matthew presents the eight beatitudes at the beginning of his gospel (Mt 5:1-11). John has only two. Here we find the first one, "If you understand this, blessed are you if you do it" (Jn 13:17). It is the beatitude of love in an extremely challenging context, immediately after the washing of the feet. At the end of his Gospel we find the beatitude of faith, "Blessed are those who have not seen and have believed" (Jn 20:29). We learn both beatitudes, faith and love, in the eucharist. It is the mystery of faith and also the mystery of love—of love to the very end. We have to grow in both. That, too, takes place in the celebration of eucharist.

Lord God,
you are not far above us
and beyond our reach.
The place you seek in this world
is neither prominent
nor exalted.
You went the way of all seed.
You are as ordinary
and as inconspicuous as bread
and, like bread,
so necessary to life.
We ask you
to let us find strength to tread this path,
to let us be for each other
as fertile as seed
and as nourishing as bread
today and every day,
forever and ever.

EIGHT

Attentiveness—the foundation of love

Jesus tells us, "It was not you who chose me, but I who chose you and appointed you to go and bear fruit that will remain" (Jn 15:16). That fruit must be of love, because love alone endures, love alone counts in the end, when our life will be judged according to love. The commandment of love is also what Jesus gave us at the Last Supper as his last will and desire: "I give you a new commandment: love one another. As I have loved you, so you also should love one another. This is how all will know that you are my disciples, if you have love for one another" (Jn 13:34-35). It is *the* command-ment of Jesus, encapsulating the whole message of his life. In that same vein, St. Paul writes, "For the whole law is fulfilled in one statement, namely, 'You shall love your neighbor as yourself'" (Gal 5:14). After Paul described at great length the various gifts and functions and services in the church, he adds, "But I shall show you a still more excellent way" (1 Cor 12:31). With that begins the great song of love. Thérèse of Lisieux, our latest and youngest doctor of the church, under-stood herself to be called by God to "be love in the heart of the Church." Ignatius of Loyola concludes his thirty-day

Spiritual Exercises with a contemplation to obtain love; he starts with the opening remark, "Love should show itself more in deeds than in words." He may imply also: more in deeds than in feelings.

Yet before the deeds comes something else, namely attentiveness, pure perception. That is the wisdom of the contemplatives. The first question is not: What can I *do* about it, but how do I *look at* it? Everything depends on our way of perceiving. Simone Weil, who penetrated deeply into this truth, sees in pure attentiveness the heart of prayer, the heart of love for God, and also the heart of love for neighbor. We need an attentive regard in which we empty ourselves of ourselves in order to reverently receive the other—be that God or our neighbor. The poet Stephen Mitchell describes prayer as "a quality of attention that makes so much room for the given, that it can appear as gift." Lovingly allowing otherness, wholly as it is, in all its truth, is extraordinarily difficult because it presupposes magnanimous self-forgetfulness. Our spontaneous perception is always related to ourselves, and therefore somewhat distorted.

To behold the other in his or her truth is the starting point of love; it cannot be omitted. Without this truthful beholding, all our further love rests shakily on a weak foundation. We need enormous discipline to let go of our stereotypes, our own advantages, and our expectations in order to behold the other as she really is. Normally, we perceive quite selectively; our filters obscure our beholding. We do not see the other in *his* reality, but distorted through *our* perception. Pure attentiveness means not favoring any aspect, rejecting nothing, and judging nothing. It also means relinquishing all anxiety for self-affirmation, all curiosity, and all criticism. The contemplatives have always known this. Modern psychology has rediscovered it.

I find impressive the pure attentiveness with which a good therapist beholds the client: unprejudiced, open minded, respectful, and without judging. Perhaps that is the most important gift of the therapist. We may need to revive this gift in our church today. In our circles, we are quick to make assessments of others, though perhaps they remain unspoken, and maybe we are even unaware of doing it.

It is best to first listen to others before we attempt to help them. Being with the poor and the marginal means, in the first place, taking them seriously as fellow human beings, letting them be our neighbors. This means literally to come closer to them, and not to stay aloof with pity or embarrassment. It means we behold, with the eyes of the heart, each human being individually in the uniqueness of their person and their life history. It means we let them speak about how they are doing. We listen carefully. We take them seriously. Unfortunately, sometimes we try to impose our "good" works on others. We may think we know what is good for the other without asking him, really. That is not genuine charity. Our own ego plays far too great a role there. St. Francis of Assisi was moved by genuine charity when he literally reversed his steps after having passed by a leper, horrified and fearful of infection. But then all of a sudden it dawned on him what he had done, and his heart was touched with a deep remorse; he turned, went back to the leper, and kissed him. So the new life of St. Francis began when he encountered a *brother* in the poor and outcast. It is so easy to measure the other with the measure of our own norms. Without realizing it we impose our own standards on everyone else. We evaluate the other according to our own ego, which is an extremely egocentric way of acting. When we can recognize and relinquish this tendency, then we may be able to encounter the other in her own dignity and truth, and in doing so we transcend our own ego. This is equally necessary in our relationship with God, who is "always greater," in the most dynamic meaning of the word. In this way, we can better grasp why Jesus always put the second commandment "you shall love your neighbor as yourself," on a par with the first: "you shall love the Lord, your God. . . ." Both commandments intend that we outgrow more and more our own ego and thus come to our true self, by loving God and loving our neighbor. Both ways require unselfish attentiveness.

For Teresa of Avila the relationships within a community are often a clearer indication of one's relationship with God than the heights of mystical prayer. She knew what she was talking about. She herself had experienced profound mystical prayer. And yet, she claims that the interactions with others are a more reliable indicator of one's relationship with God.

In fact, we find this same wisdom in the first letter of John: "If someone who has worldly means sees a brother [or sister] in need and refuses them compassion, how can the love of God remain in [that person]? . . . Whoever is without love does not know God, for God is love. . . . No one has ever seen God. Yet, if we love one another, God remains in us, and his love is brought to perfection in us" (1 Jn 3:17, 4:8, 4:12). Our first and most fundamental act of love is to behold the other in his or her otherness, without renouncing our own self, but also without absolutizing it.

Anthony de Mello tells the story of a journalist who wants to write a book about a guru. Therefore, he pays him a visit and begins with the question, "People say you are a genius. Are you?" "You might say so," the guru answered none too modestly. But the journalist—who was not particularly shy either—immediately fired another question, "And what makes one a genius?" The guru responded, "The ability to see." With this response the journalist was at a loss and helplessly mumbled, "To see what?" The guru quietly answered, "The butterfly in a caterpillar, the eagle in an egg, the saint in a selfish person." Whoever sees this is a genius, a genius in love. He picks up what is hidden in the other and is able through his loving way of looking to call it forth.[1] "To reveal to a person his or her own beauty" is how Jean Vanier defines love. Jesus had a special gift for this. He created a climate in which people could unfold themselves, in which they discovered the good they carried in themselves.

In the last Easter letter before his death, Bishop Klaus Hemmerle of Aachen wrote, "I wish each of us Easter eyes, able to perceive in death, life; in guilt, forgiveness; in separation, unity; in wounds, glory; in the human, God; in God, the human; and in the I, the You."

What we are most familiar with, we are the least likely to notice. There was a couple married for more than fifty years, sitting quietly next to each other in a train. A young couple entered and took the seats in front of them. Occasionally the young man kissed his girlfriend. The older woman watched with delight. All of a sudden she whispered to her husband, "You could do that too, for a change." But he retorted indignantly, "What is the matter with you? I don't know her at all."

In a beautiful book about the last year of her husband's life, while he was dying from cancer, the French author Anne Philipe writes, "We know each other so well that each of us can finish the sentence which the other begins, and yet the least of his gestures has more mystery in it than the smile of the Mona Lisa." That is love! After having lived together for many years, we can recognize the other from his step, and half a word is enough to understand what he wants to say. But I hope also that the other half is true for us: that we keep sensing the mystery of the other, that which we do not know and grasp. If the sense and the respect for this mystery are gone, then love has died.

In the ten commandments we are admonished not to carve idols of God; God is too great to be captured in an image. Perhaps the same holds for our neighbor.[2] We should not make an image of our neighbor, because God is the deepest mystery in each person. It is wrong to think that we can capture the other in an image. If we do so, we bypass the reality of the other person; we deal only with her image and no longer with her true self. Concluding that we "know" the other spells the end of love. That is so striking with Anne Philipe: that she knows her husband very well, yet he remains for her a great mystery. When respect for this mystery ebbs, love begins to die.

Cause and effect, however, may relate differently from what we are inclined to believe. It is not because we know the other so well that our love comes to an end. That would mean that when I really came to know the other my eyes were opened, and therefore my love cooled down. To think that is to indulge in an illusion. The real sequence of cause and effect is the reverse. Because our love has exhausted itself—has lost its vigor and warmth—the other is finished for us. We give up. *Our* love has reached its limit. Therefore, we create an image of the other. We lack the desire or the stamina to relate to the living other, day after day and year after year. It is easier to make ourselves an image of the other. In doing so we give the other notice that we are no longer willing to deal with any further growth. We box the other in and refuse him the prerogative to which every living being is entitled, namely, to change and to surprise us. And then we are amazed and disappointed that the relationship is no longer viable.

Whenever we carve representations of other persons (and we do it all the time!), we have stopped relating to them as they are, stopped beholding them in their uniqueness. We have blocked the way to seeing as God longs for us to see. We have settled for less. And the consequences affect our communities, our families, our friendships, and our workplaces.

"To love anyone is to hope in him always," says Charles de Foucauld.

> From the moment in which we begin to judge anyone, to limit our confidence in him/her, from the moment at which we identify the person with what we know of him and so reduce him to that, we cease to love the person and he ceases to be able to become better. We should expect everything of everyone. We must dare to *be love* in a world that does not know how to love.

Indeed, to relate in this way is highly unusual. The gospel challenges us to a quality of relationships far beyond the ordinary.

Sometimes we are asked to evaluate a person. That should happen in a competent and objective way. Then it is all right. In our day-to-day living, however, our opinion is often anything but objective and competent. Then our own feelings easily take center stage and result in comparing, competition, envy, annoyance, and projection.

Throughout the better part of the twentieth century, it seems that repression was the paramount defense mechanism. When a person could not cope with a problem, then it was quickly repressed into the subconscious. It was swept under the carpet and seemed to be gone. But in the subconscious it proliferated, leading to all manner of surprising, negative phenomena. Entering the twenty-first century, however, a new defense mechanism appears to be gaining ground—namely, projection. Through projection we burden someone else with our own problems. It is a far more aggressive way to cope with our own problems than was repression. Also in this case the interaction with the other person is far from competent and objective. To mention a simple example: when I, myself, am impatient, then I easily find traces of impatience in the other, and I get greatly upset. It is intolerable that that person has so little patience! Because I cannot handle my own impatience, I strike out against it in the other. We see with excessive clarity in the other what we cannot abide in ourselves, and do so subconsciously. Jesus sharply denounces such projection in his Sermon on the Mount: "Why do you notice the splinter in your brother's [or sister's] eye, but do not perceive the wooden beam in your own eye?" (Mt 7:3). Perhaps we notice sometimes that our reactions are out of proportion—that is very often a clear sign of projection. When we dislike a person too much or extol a person too much, then we are not dealing with the other person but with aspects of ourselves in the other.

When the New Testament, and especially Jesus himself, forbids us more than once to judge or to condemn, it does not refer to a situation in which a competent and objective evaluation is required, but rather to those cases in which we assess the other unwisely and unfairly. "Stop judging, that you may not be judged. For as you judge, so will you be judged, and the measure with which you measure will be measured out to you" (Mt 7:1-2). Luke's gospel adds, "Stop condemning and you will not be condemned" (Lk 6:37). In his letter to the Romans, St. Paul writes, "Why then do you judge your brother [or sister]? Or you, why do you look down on your brother [or sister]? For we shall all stand before the judgment seat of God" (Rom 14:10). The good news forbids us time and time again from judging. And yet in ecclesiastical circles this happens quite often. It almost looks like an aberration: an obsessive tendency to judge. We have, no doubt, a very extensive network of detailed norms and rules; if we use them to judge another, then we act contrary to the gospel. Moreover, we can make enormous mistakes in this regard. If we are not unselfish enough and free enough, if we do not lovingly behold the other as other, then we commit an injustice against the other person.

There is a story which might help us to be careful in judging or drawing hasty conclusions. In Germany there are fast food places where one may stand at high tables to eat. A woman goes into such a place for a quick lunch. She buys a bowl of soup and a sausage sandwich which she carefully carries to an empty table. She places the soup on the table, hangs her purse underneath, and then realizes that she has forgotten a spoon. She returns to the counter to pick up a spoon and a napkin, which she had also forgotten. When she goes back to her table, lo and behold, a stranger is happily spooning her soup. He doesn't look like a German; his dark complexion suggests an origin in Italy, Greece, or perhaps Turkey. And that man is eating her soup! First, she is flabbergasted. Then, seconds later, an enormous anger takes hold of her; she could have killed him on the spot! Another ten seconds later, she has pulled herself together and decides: he is brazen—well, so am I! She resolutely strides to the opposite side of the table and starts eating from the same bowl. One would expect that the man would apologize and disappear. Far from it. He quietly continues to eat, smiling. Apparently he does not understand German, so verbal communication is impossible. But he is extremely friendly and his smile is his weapon. He is not in the least bit intimidated. The strongest provocation comes when he offers her half of her own sausage. At the end of this awkwardly shared meal, he even extends his hand to her. By now she has calmed down enough to accept his handshake.

He leaves, and she reaches for her purse. It is gone! She had known it from the beginning—that he was a thief, and now he even stole her purse. She runs to the door, but he has disappeared. She finds herself in a very hopeless situation; her credit cards, driver's license, and all her money were all stolen. Helplessly, she scans the room and then discovers, at the adjacent table, a bowl of soup (by now cold), a sausage sandwich (untouched) and her purse hanging underneath! During all that time it had never occurred to her that it might be possible that *she, not he*, was mistaken.

Reflection on our own lives will surely provide other examples of how easily we, convinced of our own right, fail to perceive the real truth of a situation.

Lord Jesus Christ,
make us serve you and others
without pushing ourselves forward,
so that we may help our fellow men and
women
without humiliating them.
Make us dedicate ourselves
to everything that is lowly
and unimportant in the world's eyes,
so that we may do the things
that no one else takes on.
Teach us to wait, to listen
and not to speak prematurely.
Make us humble and poor enough
to accept help from others.
Send us on our way
in search of your name,
today and every day,
forever and ever.

NINE

Respect—the heart of love

Let me quote at great length Jean Vanier to explore the vital topic of love somewhat more deeply, from a different angle. Vanier is the son of a former governor of Canada, was a navy officer during World War II, and taught philosophy at the university level. The turning point in his life was when he gave up everything in order to live with two developmentally disabled men. They required all his time and all his energy. Of course, he never knew nor even suspected that this decision marked the beginning of what would later become a world-wide movement. All he wanted to do was dedicate his life to these two people who needed a great deal of assistance with daily functioning. His book, *Jesus, the Gift of Love*, has become very significant in my own life.[1]

In this book Vanier's experience with mentally disabled adults plays a very central role. For many years he lived with these people day and night, and he reflected deeply on these experiences. One of his basic convictions is that we are all disabled! Some have disabilities in their head, others in their heart, some in their eyes or in their knees or in their psyche, but we all have disabilities. Vanier would never accept the statement, "In L'Arche (the name of the movement which he founded) disabled and normal people live together." Such a sentence would negate the underlying tenet which his life experience taught him. It would contradict the heart of his mission. In the following pages which I quote directly from Vanier, he articulates the foundation of this conviction.

As children we have all been hurt.
Our first experience of pain
was on that day when, as a little child,
we sensed that we were not wanted by our
    parents,
when they were angry with us
because we did not fit into their plan
or do what they wanted us to do.
We cried out and disturbed them
when they did not want to be disturbed
or we did something that annoyed them.
We were so little, so vulnerable then,
so in need of love and of understanding.
We could not understand
that this breakage came from the fatigue,
    emptiness,
inner pain, and wounds of our parents
who could not bear to hear our cry,
and that it was not "our" fault.

We had to escape, then, into dreams,
    projects, and ideas.
When little children are hurt,
they close themselves up,
hiding behind unexpressed anger, revolt, and
    grief,
sulking in depression,
or they escape into a world of dreams.
This breakage is like a dagger
entering a fragile heart,

craving for communion.
It causes horrible loneliness, anguish, inner
    pain,
feelings of guilt and shame.
Children feel they have hurt their parents
and have disappointed them.
No child can understand or bear this inner
pain.
Children cannot judge or condemn their
    parents,
whom they need so much
just to survive.
So they withhold and hide their anger
and blame themselves.
They know then that they are no good,
unlovable,
misfits that nobody wants.

Human beings learn to cut themselves off
from all this inner pain,
and thus from reality,
and especially from the reality of people
who cause or reawaken inner pain.
We are *all* so broken in love, and in our
    capacity to relate.
We have difficulty understanding others
and wanting their growth and peace of heart.
We can quickly judge or condemn them.
We push them away,
frightened of them.
We hurt each other.
We seek to control or to use others,
or to run away and hide.

Since we were little children we have hidden
     this pain
deep down within us,
in a forgotten world
with solid barriers around it.
It is in this forgotten world
of early pain, rejection, and confusion
that the thirst for love and communion
is wounded,
and then relationships become dangerous.
So we tend to live not in reality
but in dream, in ideologies, and illusions,
in theories and projects,
things that bring success and acclaim.
The barriers around our hearts are deep and
     strong,
protecting us from pain.
We live in the past
or in the future
or in a dream.

We are all wounded people. Therefore, we are all a burden to ourselves *and* to others. Let me repeat: we burden ourselves and we burden those with whom we interact. There is
no getting around this. We simply must accept it. We must let
ourselves be healed by others, and be open to healing, correc-
tion, and deeper self-knowledge. We must also accept others
without condescension as wounded people, bear with them,
and contribute to their healing.

Not the perfect, but the imperfect implores our love.
Teresa of Avila said that she learned the most from her enemies. She said this even though she enjoyed many warm, intimate, and glorious friendships. Her point, of course, was that
she learned to love because that is the only thing that counts
and endures. From my enemies I have learned most of all how

to love. Sometimes we have to live or work closely with a person who is hard on us or gets on our nerves. How does God view that? God says that it can and should become a grace. "We know that all things work for good for those who love God, who are called according to his purpose" (Rom 8:28). God wants our contact with this difficult person to work for good. It should become something beautiful. St. Thérèse of Lisieux often repeated, especially toward the end of her life, that *all is grace*. This difficult person, then, is also a grace, as is the fact that we have come together. That should turn into a precious gift for both of us and for others. Alas, neither the gospels nor the letter to the Romans give us directions as to how to go about it. How this is going to occur remains to be seen. We are invited to be creative and inventive here. St. Paul's affirmation that *all things work together for good* can bolster our confidence—after all, it's no less than a divine guarantee! Thus we can start off with the certainty that God assures us, "It can be done."

Let us approach the same theme in a more practical way. If a person limps, we naturally assume that the person has trouble with his leg or hip, preventing him from walking normally. Spontaneously we are ready to help and to have patience with that person. It also happens, however, that someone goes through life limping, psychologically. Then we can be just as certain that something is slightly out of order. It may be only a little thing, but this deficiency forces the person to act differently. In order to survive, in order to cope with life, he has to do it limping.

Now it is striking that with a physically limping person, we usually have much understanding and good will. But with a psychologically limping person we can sometimes be harsh. We cannot stand it that this person has this hang up. He must change. We exert pressure, sometimes in a very imprudent way. We may even be cruel, probably without realizing it ourselves. The only thing that can bring us to a more lenient approach would be if the person admits that he has psychological problems. Then we are ready to show pity.

Strange! From a limping person we do not demand that he first give us a declaration of his disability. How much more fruitful it would be if we would instead quietly reflect on how to turn this situation to the good. That is what God intends.

"The greatest thing on earth is respect, because it is the heart of love." Once when I was on vacation, I read this sentence on the tabernacle of a village church. The text annoyed me because it sounded like a glib commercial. After my visit to that church, I went for a long walk in the woods, and though I did not like these words, they kept nagging me. Running out of patience, I finally asked myself what I considered to be the greatest thing on earth. The answer was self-evident: Love is the greatest thing on earth. Only then did it dawn on me that this text also spoke of love, in a very specific way: it pointed out that *respect* is the heart of love. With this insight, my mood changed and I started to think about the text with a positive attitude. Much to my surprise, I discovered a gem. Now I am convinced that where respect is absent, love is lacking. We can give someone in need a thousand dollars, but if we do it without respect, we insult or hurt the person because love is lacking. Also, in our interactions with one another this is true: if there is no respect, then there is no love. This applies to all relationships, no matter what kind of disability we are dealing with—be it physical or psychological—or whether or not we have trouble with the person. Every person is entitled to our respect because therein our love crystallizes itself.

During his public life Jesus often mentioned that love for our neighbor, though it is the second commandment, is equal to the love of God, the first great commandment. "You shall love the Lord, your God, with all your heart, with all your soul, and with all your mind. This is the greatest and the first commandment. The second is like it: You shall love your neighbor as yourself" (Mt 22:37-39). It is beautiful that the second commandment is so intimately connected with the first one. But there is also a certain tragedy in the fact that the measure of our charity is the measure of our self-love. Indeed, that is the natural boundary. We cannot love our neighbor more than we love ourselves. Sadly, quite a few people do not love themselves very much. In the spirit of Carl Gustav Jung we can make a distinction between egoism and self-love. The former is love for the ego, and therefore not very open towards others. Self-love is more mature, more capable of loving our neighbors. To spoil oneself is a form of egoism and usually a sign that self-love has not yet developed properly. Similarly, parents who spoil a child are often looking more for their own benefit than for the real good of their child.

The gospel calls us, quoting Leviticus, to love our neighbor as ourselves. People who truly love themselves are also able to love their neighbor. If our self-love is limited, we are easily inclined to seek our own self-affirmation and a stronger sense of self-worth in our contacts with others. In these cases, what passes for love may well contain a fair amount of egoism.

It is remarkable that towards the end of his life Jesus goes far beyond the norm of self love. In fact, he makes an enormous leap. He really teaches something quite new. "I give you a new commandment: love one another. As I have loved you, so you also should love one another. This is how all will know that you are my disciples, if you have love for one another" (Jn 13:34-35). The measure for our charity is no longer "love your neighbor as yourself," but "love your neighbor *as I love*." What an enormous difference! We do not need much reflection to realize that this challenges us entirely beyond our ability. To love one another as Jesus has loved us! Do we have to wash each other's feet, then? Are we to pray for our persecutors when we suffer injustice, "Father, forgive them, they know not what they do"? Must we call our Judas, "friend"? All of this, obviously, is completely beyond us.

Of course, Jesus knew very well that in this farewell command he was demanding something from us which we cannot accomplish on our own. "As I have loved you, so you also should love one another." Such love is possible only if it is

given to us. Here we touch a very essential element of the
gospel: God is love and the source of all love. What we have
to do is open our hearts in order to let the love of God flow in
and fill us. Then, when our hearts are filled with that love of
God, the love runs over and we pass on what we have
received. The stream is God's love for us; it flows through us
to become our love for our neighbor. It is the same stream,
springing from one and the same source.

Recall again the analogy of the Jordan. If our hearts are
closed, they become like the Dead Sea—so salty that in and
around it nothing can live. But if we open our hearts so that
the love of God can flow in and out, they become like a Sea
of Galilee teeming with life and freshness. The love with
which we love must be given to us; we have to receive it from
God, take it in and pass it on. It is our task to make our hearts
wide, receptive, and open for such love.

The geography of my home country, Holland, provides a
charming analogy. At the village of Wijk bij Duurstede, the
Rhine changes its name. This I learned as a child in grade
school, and my imagination conjured up an impressive monu-
ment of nature simply because this mighty river changed its
name, as if that alone caused it to be a different river. When I
later happened to visit the place, I discovered that it was an
unspectacular, down-to-earth place. All that designates that
place as unique is a sign which says that the river from that
point on is named Lek.

The river is the same as it was before it reached this
place. Only our name for it has changed. Jesus' great new
commandment of love of neighbor is also simpler than our
imaginations might think. There is only one stream of love,
which originates from God and flows through us to our
neighbor. When the stream reaches our heart, it changes its
name. First, it is God's love for us, then it is our love of our
neighbor. To put it still more succinctly: the love which Jesus
demands from us, he himself is already giving us. That is a
basic pattern of all life according to the gospel. In many ways
the gospel utterly exceeds our capacity, if we strive to live it

on our own strength. But the art of living the gospel lies precisely in letting God work in and through us. This requires our complete dedication, but at the same time such a life is relaxed and full of a peace which the world does not know.

In the thirteenth chapter of his first letter to the Corinthians, St. Paul sings the Song of Love. In the middle of it he offers a phenomenology of love. Paul meticulously describes here what love looks like, by sketching a portrait of Jesus: "Love is patient, love is kind. It is not jealous, [love] is not pompous . . . " (1 Cor 13:4). If we replace the word 'love' with the name of Jesus, then it fits perfectly: "Jesus is patient, Jesus is kind. He is not jealous, is not pompous, he is not inflated, he is not rude, he does not seek his own interests, he is not quick-tempered, he does not brood over injury, he does not rejoice over wrongdoing but rejoices with the truth. He bears all things, believes all things, hopes all things, endures all things." In the person of Jesus we experience what love is. It is good to gaze often at Jesus and to learn from him about this stream of love, which God so desires will flow in us. Elsewhere St. Paul writes, "I live, no longer I, but Christ lives in me" (Gal 2:20). We could paraphrase, "I love, but it is not I who loves, it is Christ who loves in me." All that matters in our life is love—love alone counts and endures. What love really is we must learn from Jesus. He alone can awaken this love in us and enable it to flourish.

The other is also wounded.
You have mercy with the inability of both of us.
Therefore, give me the good will
to see the need of the other
and not to nurse my own wounds
like a dark treasure
which occupies my mind continuously.
The other is also wounded.
You see through the reasons
why we did not listen to the signals of our heart.
Prevent me from bargaining for myself
the deeper pain,
the smaller part of our guilt
as profit to which I am not entitled.
The other is also wounded,
and when I seek his presence,
then you, God, are with us both.
I want to begin seeing him,
whom the anger alienated from me so much,
with your eyes.
Lord, restore the shattered confidence
and when I cannot forgive,
then please forgive in me.
I pray for your peace
which puts an end to all enmity.
Lord, say to us both:
peace be with you
today and every day,
forever and ever![2]

TEN

"Father, forgive them . . ."

Let us now take time to be present at Golgotha and there meditate on the first of Jesus' final words from the cross, "Father, forgive them, they know not what they do" (Lk 23:34).

The Old Testament mentions several times that God hears the poor when they cry and even when they curse.

> A beggar in distress do not reject;
>   avert not your face from the poor.
> From the needy turn not your eyes,
>   give no man reason to curse you;
> for if in the bitterness of his soul he curse you,
>   his Creator will hear his prayer.
>
> —Sirach 4:4-6

Exodus proclaims in the same way, "You shall not molest or oppress an alien, for you were once aliens yourselves in the land of Egypt. You shall not wrong any widow or orphan. If ever you wrong them and they cry out to me, I will surely hear their cry" (Ex 22:20-22).

How much more, then, will God listen to the cry of his Son, who has emptied himself to the point of utter poverty.

Moreover, the cry of Jesus is a petition full of love, "Father, forgive them, they know not what they do." Jesus pronounced forgiveness of sins on a number of occasions, here, however, he calls upon his Father to forgive.

This prayer is meant in the first place for the executioners, the Roman soldiers who actually drove the nails into his wrists and his feet. Indeed, they do not know what they are doing. They do not have the slightest idea who on this day is the victim of their usual trade.

This petition of Jesus is also meant for Pilate, who gave the order to crucify Jesus, and for those who were involved in the judgment: the scribes, the priests, and the Pharisees. Here the situation is more nuanced: they know very well which order they gave; they planned it carefully and carried it out meticulously. On a deeper level, however, the petition rings true: they do not know what they are doing. They did not know the mission and the person of Jesus, and above all his relationship with his Abba and his immense love. They had closed off their hearts.

Finally, this prayer of Jesus applies also to us: "Father, forgive them, they know not what they do." If we want to know Jesus better, to love him more, and to follow him more closely, then we must now gaze intently, listen carefully, and open our hearts widely. We have a unique chance to come closer to Jesus by contemplating his prayer for forgiveness.

The teaching of Jesus is that we should forgive one another. In the sermon on the plain Jesus says, "Forgive and you will be forgiven" (Lk 6:37). In the Our Father he teaches us to pray, "Forgive us our trespasses as we forgive those who trespass against us." The little word "as" carries an explosive charge.

Once Peter asked Jesus, "Must I forgive my brother as many as seven times?" Jesus answered, "I say to you, not seven times but seventy-seven times" (Mt 18:22). In the Jewish idiom this means without restriction. In addition to this answer, Jesus tells the parable of the man with an excessively great debt, an amount surpassing all imaginable proportions.

When this man pleads, "Be patient with me, and I will pay you back in full," both he and his master know that this promise is out of the question. Nevertheless, the master forgave him the loan. Immediately afterwards this same man seized a colleague who owed him a much smaller amount. Rightly, the master summoned him back reproaching him, "You wicked servant! I forgave you your entire debt because you begged me to. Should you not have had pity on your fellow servant, as I had pity on you?" The point of this parable seems to be not so much a moral demand— since God has forgiven us, we must forgive our neighbor—but rather an existential necessity. If our hearts are not completely hardened and if we realize, even a little bit, how much has been forgiven us, we cannot help forgiving our neighbor. If we do not do the latter, then we apparently have not grasped the truth of our forgiveness.

Human forgiveness means that the person forgiving overcomes his grudge and resentment. In this way his own heart is freed and relieved. Cardinal Bernardin gave a beautiful example of this.

> God's grace has helped me both survive the trying time [of my false accusation] and deepen my understanding of what it means to forgive even those who hurt us most. During those months I emptied myself more than I ever had so that God could take over. As a result, my reconciliation with [my accuser] filled me with new life.[1]

Divine forgiveness is totally different. In this case nothing changes in God who forgives, but only in the person who receives forgiveness. The heart of the person *forgiven* thaws, loses its protective crust, and is fully revived.

Luke recounts an event that illustrates this in a striking way: the encounter of the sinful woman with Jesus in the house of Simon the Pharisee. In this passage we find a verse that has caused the exegetes much trouble. The first edition of the *New American Bible* translates it, "I tell you, that is why her many sins are forgiven—because of her great love" (Lk 7:47). When taken out of context, probably everyone would understand the verse this way: her many sins are forgiven because she showed such a great love; through her love she obtained forgiveness. Of course, this cannot be correct because this interpretation directly contradicts the previous parable, where Jesus proclaims that being forgiven leads to greater gratitude and love. Moreover, such an interpretation would be out of sync with the whole of scripture, which always presents God's forgiveness as a free gift, a grace which we cannot earn. The second edition of the *New American Bible* more accurately translates this verse, "So I tell you, her many sins have been forgiven; hence, she has shown great love." Though in this translation the subtle ambiguity of the Greek text is sacrificed, an obvious and common misunderstanding has been eliminated. The message is now unmistakable: the very great love of this woman is the *fruit* of the forgiveness which she experienced so intensely. When she saw Jesus, she immediately knew in her heart that he forgave her guilt. The loving gaze of Jesus was completely different from the stares of those who wanted her favors, as well as from the dismissive scrutiny of the condemning and rejecting Pharisees. Under the tender look of Jesus the thick ice crust around her heart melted like snow in the sun. Her love was set free, and it proved to be expansive. She lavished her love on Jesus exuberantly. The forgiveness of Jesus had liberated her love from its confinement. Love blossomed as the fruit of forgiveness.

Both the teaching and the practice of Jesus show us time and time again his inexhaustible willingness to forgive. To the woman caught in adultery, Jesus says, "Has no one condemned you? . . . Neither do I condemn you" (Jn 8:10-11). The chief tax collector, Zaccheus, was privileged to experience salvation coming to his own house because the Son of Man had come to seek out and to save what was lost (see Lk 19:9-10). The paralytic who was lowered through the roof was startled when Jesus announced, "Your sins are forgiven;" that is not what he had come for (see Mk 2:1-12). Over and over, Jesus forgave. He did not necessarily wait for the admission of guilt or for signs of contrition, as the example of the paralytic shows. What Jesus tells us in the parable of the prodigal son and the re-found father, he had first lived himself: "Whoever sees me, sees the Father." Forgiveness is the completion of love. Forgiveness implies a willingness to suffer from the other person without writing him off.

What does this stance of Jesus mean for us, for me personally? The Word of God who is love, has become flesh. Jesus incarnates God's forgiveness. With his whole person and all through his life—especially in the "hour" when he dies on the cross—Jesus let us know and experience that his forgiveness is without limits and his love excludes no one. This Word is also my salvation. "With you is forgiveness and on this we live." We should take here a long pause to absorb this message, to let it envelop us and take root in us. The Father heard the prayer of the dying Jesus, turning his awful death into a source of forgiveness of all guilt.

The next phase, however, inevitably comes: Do I have to forgive someone else? Violence and aggression have become rampant in our day. Forgiveness must divert this rising tide of violence, or rather stanch its flow. During Easter of 1961 Dag Hammarskjöld, the second Secretary General of the United Nations, wrote in his diary, "Forgiveness breaks the chain of causality." Hatred causes and justifies violence, and violence in turn stirs up hatred. That is a vicious cycle, a satanic circle. Forgiveness breaks this cycle open. Our world desperately needs forgiveness. Without forgiveness it is losing its human face and the reflection of its Creator.

Forgiveness does not imply glossing over or making excuses. We will never truly forgive if we have not honestly acknowledged how wrong the other was to hurt us.

Forgiveness does not mean to repress, to try to forget. That is neither genuine forgiveness nor a true solution. The saying goes, "To forgive and to forget." Though I hold much popular wisdom in high esteem, I do not quite agree in this case. Whenever a profound injustice is done to us, it remains engraved in our memory, sometimes even in our body, and certainly in our psyche. We cannot forget it. That would be asking the impossible, and I do not believe this should be our ideal.

Nor is forgiveness a harmless naïveté which waters things down, pretends there has been no harm and then tries to smooth things over. That is not genuine forgiveness. Forgiveness is not a lack of backbone, a tendency to avoid any confrontation, without conviction and without true connectedness, an indulgence stemming from a lack of courage. All these are caricatures which put us on the wrong track.

People who do not forgive remain in the power of whoever injured them. Those with whom we choose to remain angry will control us. They will limit us emotionally, physically, developmentally, and spiritually. There is a Chinese proverb to the effect that the person who seeks revenge should dig two graves. Forgiveness is in no way a form of weakness. On the contrary, it requires a great strength.

There may be other kinds of misconceptions, too. First, there may be some misunderstanding underlying the hurt we experience. Perhaps the person hurting us intended something completely different from what we understood. There may be a mistake on our part, or on the other's part. If this misinterpretation is cleared up, we may easily reconnect with each other.

Next, we should never forget that every person is larger than his or her failings. It would be a serious injustice to reduce a person to his or her failings. That would mean to create an image of our neighbor—the image of an evil person—and to confine him in it. If what we see in the other is only his or her failings, then we have ceased relating with the other in a fair way. Every human person is greater than his or her failings.

Moreover, even if the other person is guilty, it can very well be that we, too, are guilty. It is extremely difficult to deal justly with the injustice of others. Not many of us are capable of that. When the guilt of the other is crystal clear to us, it might still be salutary to take a few minutes to reflect and to examine how we coped with that unfairness, and to ask ourselves whether we have not become guilty as well. The anger we feel at the guilt of the other can readily lead to repression of our own guilt. We then see only part of the picture, part of the truth.

Forgiveness means giving up the disappointment and the resentment to which we are entitled. We really have a reason and a right to be angry and aggrieved. Yet, we can choose not to cling to these feelings. We can sacrifice to God our resentment. The other person has truly been unfair to us, and our disappointment is altogether normal and healthy; yet we need not brood over it. We can deliberately relinquish it and encounter the person who has hurt us with more goodwill than he or she deserves according to human standards. Genuine forgiveness robs us of our hurt. We can no longer harbor it for later use against the other. We surrender the hard feelings that may have become a cherished, if bitter, possession, and thus we lose a painful advantage. We all need more love than we deserve. Forgiveness appeals to our generosity, to practice this "more" and to give other persons more love than they deserve.

Why is forgiveness often so difficult? Something in us wants to hold on to our pain and our justified bitterness. It is like a dark treasure that we wrongly consider to be precious. We cherish it. The other has been unfair and unjust to us. We dwell on it. We retreat into a corner, ensconce ourselves in it, and nurture our wounds, making ourselves impenetrable to any thought of forgiveness and love. We nurture the gloomy mystery of our pain and bitterness with a kind of addiction that wreaks havoc. Indeed, in this way we destroy our own life and ruin our happiness. This is also the point where quite a few people get stuck in their spiritual life—that they cannot forgive. They turn around in an unhealthy circle of endless repetitions to the point of becoming neurotic. Something that happened twenty years ago is dished up with a fervor and satisfaction as if it happened yesterday. Resentments have been kept alive and nurtured for decades—a vicious cycle, a deadly prison. We have turned around in that cycle so often, but we cannot get out of it; the leap into freedom keeps eluding us.

Perhaps it is the harboring of a personal failure. Some time in our life we failed, and we blame someone else for it. If the other person had behaved differently, it would have turned out for us successfully. We are unable to forgive the other this fault! Someone thwarted our plans, which had seemed so promising. We lost face and felt humiliated. And now we cling tenaciously to our disappointment. The other caused us to look silly—we are hurt in our honor or sensitivity. And the wound keeps growing larger and larger. Forgive? Nobody can expect this from us!

In forgiveness something really new breaks through in our world. Whoever wants to live creatively, must forgive. Without forgiveness we remain imprisoned—caught—in the demonic circle of endless repetitions, in a sterile and one-dimensional world far from God.

To forgive means to choose life, and not to forgive means to choose death or the many small steps towards living without happiness and without blessing. Forgiveness can renew a person, a community, and even a nation. Forgiveness is the courageous act of an alert person, who breaks through the deceptive enchantment of evil and tries to liberate even the enemy from sterile isolation. In this way forgiveness opens a new future for ourselves and for the other. Not to forgive makes relationships peter out. We turn around in the cold confines of bitterness, self-pity, and contempt for others. Not to forgive severs communication and isolates a person. We lose contact with our fellow men and women and eventually with reality. Ultimately, justice does not consist in destroying the evil person (as with capital punishment), but in liberating him or her from destructiveness and in offering the possibility of new relationships. Only forgiveness can open up a real future and create new connections. Violence can never achieve this. Whoever seeks the downfall of his opponents—humiliation, failure, defeat, misfortune, unhappiness—has not yet understood the gospel. Whoever wants the eradication of his enemies—in concentration camps, ethnic cleansing, inquisition, capital punishment—closes off the future and renders God's world uninhabitable.

Forgiveness is the free act of an independent person who does not let herself be forced into the logic of her opponent. It is, no doubt, very difficult to forgive. But *not to forgive* may be even more difficult. Then bitterness and resentment poison our own life. It is a gift and a liberation to be able to forgive. Forgiveness is essential to love as Jesus understands it, love that "does not brood over injury" (1 Cor 13:5).

Whoever really wants to forgive has to come down from his throne. Otherwise, the attempt at forgiveness degenerates into an indictment and then we should not be surprised when the other person rejects the offer. In order to forgive in freedom and love, we need inner truthfulness and a good amount of humility. Sometimes reconciliation is impossible, not because of the obduracy and hardness of heart of the wrongdoer, but because of the pride and haughtiness of the wronged person. Forgiveness is a gradual realization that we cannot control another.

Forgiveness is hard work in our heart and mind, especially if we have to forgive our parents or supervisors, clergy or friends. Moreover, forgiveness is both a decision and a long process. We cannot do it all at once. We have to forgive many times before our heart becomes truly free. The analogy of a spiral could be helpful here (and in many other cases as well). We can turn around in a circle without making any progress, but if we move in a spiral, then in each round we ascend a little higher. So there is progress, albeit slow. The point of the comparison, however, is that in a spiral motion we pass the same point in every orbit and are confronted with the same view. We have to come to grips with it every time. And then we can move on to another round until we once more return to the same point. Then we have to forgive again. Such is life. We cannot forgive in one grand act, but only in a continuing process.

At the end of chapter five, it was mentioned that the *acceptance* of forgiveness is a process. But forgiveness itself is also a process. We must be willing and courageous and tenacious enough to forgive time and time again. We can distinguish in this process several phases. First, there must grow in us a fundamental willingness to forgive. In the second phase the desire to forgive grows, but it all takes place in our intellect and will power; the heart is not yet tuned in. That means that we are on the way, that we have reached a higher level, but not yet the goal itself. Then gradually we move into the third phase in which the forgiveness really comes from the heart, in which the bitterness disappears and we become much more transparent.

All three phases are grace. On our own strength, we are not capable of really forgiving, especially if it concerns deep hurt. Forgiving is the most divine thing we can do. It is the completion of love. When we notice that we cannot (yet) forgive, we must be very much on our guard not to blame ourselves or to get discouraged, so long as there is a sincere desire to grow towards forgiveness. Discouragement is always the work of an evil spirit.

The best thing to do now is to go and sit beneath a crucifix, quietly contemplating Jesus, all the while hearing his prayer, "Father, forgive them, they know not what they do."

How many thoughts there are in my heart,
my God,
which sow destruction!
I sense the anger,
the coldness,
the rage,
the urge to strike back.
I let all this surface,
but it does not relieve me.
I want to protect
the person who has hurt me
from myself.
I want to understand him,
to perceive his need
and to remember
all I owe him.
I want to forgive.
Is my love so feeble
that it cannot accept to be wounded?
And, have I not myself
wounded the other?
I will not allow
implacability to take root in me.

God,
you are generous in forgiving.
Heal us,
bring us again on the way
to one another
and to you,
today and every day,
forever and ever.[2]

ELEVEN

The crucified Jesus

In some Christian regions there are villages where the church bells are rung each Friday at three o'clock in the afternoon. They remind us of an immensely significant hour in human history: on a Friday, the cross of Jesus was hoisted on Golgotha. This cross casts its shadow on all ages before and after it. It stands in the center of time. In Western culture we count the years before and after Christ. Not only timewise, but also geographically, the cross stands in the center of the world. All the roads of humankind keep leading to this spot. The motto of the Carthusians reads, *Stat crux, dum volvitur orbis*—the cross stands while the world turns. The cross forms the axis, the hub. Everyone meets the cross. We can, however, react in very different ways. What is my spontaneous reaction when I see a crucifix? A good question—with a revealing answer. Is my first thought an estimation of its artistic value? Romanesque or Baroque, stylish or kitsch? Or, do I immediately think of the passion and agony of Jesus? Do I recall the extreme cruelty of this most shameful way of execution in ancient times? Am I reminded of the surrender of Jesus? Of his love? What comes first to my mind when I see a crucifix? That reveals something about me.

There are many ways to react, not only to the crucifix as an image, but also to the cross as a reality—in the past when Jesus died on it, or in the present when it enters our life. Some react with bitter rejection or silent despondency. There can also be an intimate bond with the cross on which "my love is crucified." An infinite variety of reactions exist between these extremes. From the beginning the crucifix was a sign of contradiction. The one thief crucified with Jesus prays for the grace of reconciliation and for the kingdom, while the other scoffs and rejects bitterly—the same position, right and left of Jesus' cross. Some ridicule Jesus and challenge him to come down from the cross. The Roman centurion, by contrast, confesses, "Truly, this was the Son of God!" (Mt 27:54).

We all meet the cross. Our reaction to it matters. In March 1996, seven Trappist monks were cruelly slaughtered in Algeria, victims of religious fanaticism. The local bishop, Pierre Claverie, gave the homily at the funeral of these martyrs. A few months later this bishop himself was murdered by the same fundamentalists. While he preached, his own death was imminent. Was he aware of this? In this homily he said among other things,

> If Christianity distances itself from the cross, its content and strength are lost to a certain extent. The vitality of the church, its fruitfulness and hope, have their matrix and their roots in the cross of Jesus. Nowhere else! All the rest is secondary, leads to illusions and pulls the wool over our eyes. The church cheats itself and others if she acts like a worldly power, like a humanitarian organization among other humanitarian organizations, or like an enterprise of evangelization with spectacular effects.

The cross is the center of history and the center of the church. From there only comes our fruitfulness. My love is crucified. Christians are people who have recognized the Son of God in this crucified man, who have been touched by his love to the very end, and who have found in him the great love of their lives. The cross is for them the center of the world. Cyril of Jerusalem said, "God extended his arms on the cross to embrace the ends of the earth." God opened himself widely in all directions with outstretched arms desiring to encompass everybody and everything. In the words of Lactantius, an early Christian writer, "God extended his arms on the cross and embraced the whole earth in order to signify that from the rising of the sun until its setting, a future people would gather under God's wings."

At this point the whole world is at stake. In the eleventh chapter of John's gospel we find a remarkable passage. As the Sanhedrin deliberates over the death of Jesus, one of its members, Caiaphas speaks, "You know nothing, nor do you consider that it is better for you that one man should die instead of the people, so that the whole nation may not perish." Then John adds this explanation, "He did not say this on his own, but since he was high priest for that year, he prophesied that Jesus was going to die for the nation, and not only for the nation, but also to gather into one the dispersed children of God" (Jn 11:49-52). Beneath every crucifix belongs a globe.

"[I want] to know [Christ] and the power of his resurrection and [the] sharing of his sufferings by being conformed to his death, if somehow I may attain the resurrection from the dead" (Phil 3:10-11). "May I never boast except in the cross of our Lord Jesus Christ, through which the world has been crucified to me, and I to the world" (Gal 6:14). Impressive words from St. Paul, but to realize them in the daily reality of our lives is not easy. There the cross can easily trigger rejection or depression, if we see primarily its frustration and unfairness.

If someone had told me ahead of time what I am experiencing with you, my God, I would have dismissed it as frenzy. Even now while it seizes my whole being, it still transcends my understanding. I go through fire and am not burned. I carry heavy burdens, and they do not bog me down. What I had feared with great anxiety has happened, and I survived. You are with me—and I can bear the uncertainty, accept the pain. I, full of impatience, can wait confidently and surrender myself and all that is mine to you, because you fight for me. Like a seal, your doings imprint themselves in my soul, so that I shall never forget what you are capable of.[1]

Thus speaks someone who has experienced and accepted the cross in her life. But how many do not succeed in saying yes and become discontent, lose perspective, and slip into bitterness. That God revealed himself definitively in a crucified man boggles all human expectations.

In Protestant theology, especially in the school of Karl Barth, a marked distinction is drawn between religion and faith. Religion is the highest that people can reach—human beings at our greatest. Faith, by contrast, comes from God, is divine, and unattainable on our own. Faith is *given* to us by God. This theological tradition perceives a deep chasm between religion and faith. When Dietrich Bonhoeffer, for instance, speaks about "religionless" Christianity, he means pure faith without contamination of religion in the sense we just described.

In the same sense Bonhoeffer also claims—and here no one disputes him—that all religions expect a powerful God, a God who always helps us, who may not spare us the trouble of life, but does alleviate it. Faith is the great counterpart of religion. Religion counts on a mighty God, whereas faith brings us a crucified God. This faith comes as grace, which we can never attain by our own effort.

The evangelist John, like the synoptics, also mentions three predictions or summaries of the passion, but very much from his own unique perspective. The second one reads, "When you lift up the Son of Man, then you will realize that I AM . . . " (Jn 8:28). In the translation "I AM" the divine name par excellence shines through clearly: "Yahweh—I Am Who Am." This is an appalling paradox. Jesus essentially is saying, when I die on the cross like a worm, barely human, then you will recognize in me the ineffable God.

Humanly speaking, it is inexplicable that people have often and truly found God in this crucified man. Two extremely intelligent Jewish women of the twentieth century, for example, experienced this grace: Simone Weil and Edith Stein. They recognized Jesus as God while he died on the cross, of all places. Simone Weil writes in a letter to Father Perin, her spiritual director and friend, "The precious gift for me is, as you know, the cross. If it will not be given to me that I deserve to participate in the cross of Christ, then I hope at least to participate in that of the penitent thief. After Christ, of all the people mentioned in the gospel, the penitent thief is the one I envy most. During the crucifixion of Jesus, to be at his side and in the same position as he, seems to me a far more enviable privilege than to sit at his right hand in his glory" (letter of April 16, 1942). This is not pious enthusiasm. Simone Weil paid with the price of her own life.

Edith Stein also discovered, or rather re-discovered, God in the crucified Jesus. From 1916 onward, Edith Stein was assistant to Professor Edmund Husserl in Freiburg, Germany. In November 1917, the philosopher, Adolf Reinach of Goettingen, fell in the battle of Flanders. Edith made the long trip from Freiburg to Goettingen to attend the funeral, and also to pay a visit of condolence to the widow, Anna Reinach. The latter visitation was not easy for Edith because she felt incapable of speaking profound words of consolation. During the encounter, however, the roles were completely turned. It was the widow, Anna Reinach, who in all her grief was able to convey to Edith Stein something of the consolation of her faith. Later, as a Carmelite, Edith Stein speaks about this experience in these words, "This was my first encounter with the cross and the divine strength it conveys to those who carry it. I saw very clearly for the first time the church, born from the redemptive passion of Christ, in her triumph over the sting of death. It was the moment in which my unbelief collapsed, and Christ began to shine for me, Christ in the mystery of his cross." The moment in which my *unbelief* collapsed. Usually one hears: the moment my *faith* collapsed. But she says, my unbelief collapsed, as if it were like a wall that hid the mystery of the cross. Later as a Carmelite she chose her name in relation to the cross: Teresa Benedicta a Cruce—Teresa blessed by the cross.

These two women are examples of many who found the Son of God in the crucified and responded to the cross in profound faith. "When you lift up the Son of Man, then you will realize that I AM. . . . "

Jesus hangs there, expelled from the world which rejects and alienates him—he does not belong to it any more—and cut off from heaven to which he does not belong either, because "for our sake [God] made him to be sin who did not know sin" (2 Cor 5:21); an unfathomable, painful mystery. Hardly human, more like a worm.

He, the most free man ever, hangs completely bound and nailed. Everything has been taken away from him:

- His clothing, the only possession he had;
- His human dignity, while he hangs there naked, for everybody to see;
- His health, which has been ruined in just 12 hours;
- His reputation, destroyed; it is not long ago that people admired and reverenced him;
- His credibility, because scripture says, "Cursed be everyone who hangs on a tree" (Gal 3.13, quoting Dt 21:23). And now he

hangs on the tree. That is the great triumph of his opponents. This text from Deuteronomy is the biblical confirmation of their triumph;

- His friends and his disciples; at his arrest "they all left him and fled"(Mk 14:50);

- His mother, whom he entrusts to us as his last legacy, and us to her;

- His Father, and that was the worst of all: "My God, my God, why have you forsaken me?" (Mk 15:34).

Complete emptiness, absolute abandonment, utter desolation, but at the same time, a refuge for us in our loneliness, Jesus hangs between heaven and earth. He belongs to neither, but makes a bridge between the two. Jean Vanier notes how Jesus makes the transition:

- from healer to wounded;

- from a compassionate person to one who needs compassion;

- from one who exclaimed with a loud voice, "Let anyone who thirsts come to me and drink," to the one who cries, "I thirst";

- from the one who proclaims the good news to the poor to the one who has become poor himself.

Jesus links the great divide that runs through humankind separating those with plenty from those in need. Jesus hangs between heaven and earth. The evil in this world congeals into a concentration of power like a clenched fist, which strikes out at him. But precisely there the Word speaks its most clear language, the body language. Truly, "the Word has become flesh." Now we can *see* what the Word has to say. Now we can both hear and see the message of the Word. It is a message of love. "Jesus loved his own in the world and he loved them to the end" (Jn 13:1). With this sentence, John gives us not only the key to the Last Supper, but to the whole passion. This means that we only contemplate the passion of

Jesus with the right mindset and in true Christian faith, if we perceive time and time again and in every detail this love to the very end.

Let us elaborate on this in two dimensions. First, the crucifix tells us how much we are loved by God, how precious we are in God's eyes. "Only with difficulty does one die for a just person, though perhaps for a good person one might even find courage to die. But God proves his love for us in that while we were still sinners Christ died for us. . . . He who did not spare his own Son but handed him over for us all, how will he not also give us everything else along with him?" (Rom 5:7-8; 8:32).

Many people in our modern, highly technical—but often individualistic and isolating—society are desperately seeking their identity. Much energy and money is invested in this search. The archetypes of C. G. Jung can throw a light on the background of our personality. The Myers-Briggs test and the Enneagram can help us to better understand our own behavior. In popular magazines, the regular features on astrology, zodiac constellation, and horoscopes play on this need in their own way. For those who want to go deeper, there is an extensive array of workshops, seminars, and various therapies, the most intensive of which might be psychoanalysis. In the wood of these possibilities we should not overlook the tree of the cross. There, above all, we can learn how precious we are in God's eyes. If sometimes we have to cope with feelings of inferiority, then it is healthy and profitable to gaze frequently on the cross of Jesus: there we can see how much worth we have. If we find it difficult to accept ourselves—self-acceptance is a delicate art—then we can learn this art here: God shows us in Jesus how immensely valuable and loved we are. Psychotherapy delves deeper and deeper into early childhood, infancy, and if possible even into the prenatal stage. I often think we should go still a little further, to the point where we were born from God's longing. We have to go back that far. That is where the deepest dignity of our person lies. From this love we come forth. Nothing can shake it or alter it for all eternity. God's longing for us is eternally present—on God's love we live more than on air and food and drink. That is where our real roots lie, our deepest source. If we fall short, this love still remains in its entirety. That is what the cross reveals to us. That is what we can learn from the crucifix.

The second dimension is that this message of the cross does not apply only to each of us personally, but also to all others. St. Paul calls his fellow Christians "the brother [or sister] for whom Christ died" (1 Cor 8:11). That is indeed the most important thing we can say about the brother or sister: that Jesus died for him or for her. Whether or not a person is attractive, is young or old, has an advanced degree or none at all, has a great command of language or hardly any, or has a prestigious position or is at the bottom of the ladder; all this is as *nothing* compared to the fact that Jesus loved this person to the very end and died for him or her on the cross.

In our perception of our fellow human beings, we should hold this thought uppermost in our minds and hearts. Only when this basic truth permeates all our relationships can they be really Christian. The death of Jesus on the cross established among all of us a connectedness far more potent than all the distinctions we are accustomed to making. Jesus died "to gather into one the dispersed children of God" (Jn 11:52). We always have to measure the value of our neighbor in relation to the death of Jesus.

Our baptism confirms and deepens this root relationship. "Or are you unaware that we who were baptized into Christ Jesus were baptized into his death?" (Rom 6:3). We are all signed with this seal. "For all of you who were baptized into Christ have clothed yourselves with Christ. There is neither Jew nor Greek, there is neither slave nor free person, there is not male and female; for you are all one in Christ Jesus" (Gal 3:27-28). The death of Jesus on the cross teaches us to accept our fellow men and women as they are, profoundly bound to us, as we all are in Christ. The death of Jesus on the cross also teaches us that most difficult art: forgiveness.

After John relates the death of Jesus and the piercing of his side, he quotes the prophet Zechariah, "They will look upon him whom they have pierced." Immediately preceding this verse in the Book of Zechariah, we find, "I will pour out on the house of David and on the inhabitants of Jerusalem a spirit of grace and petition" (Zec 12:10). If we look on him whom we have pierced, much will be given to us. Jesus gives us his Spirit, the spirit of respect and love, the spirit in which he himself has lived. The holy Cure d'Ars used to say, "The crucifix is the most learned book a person can read." From this book he drew his wisdom and his love and his astounding fruitfulness.

The cross reveals its authentic meaning only when we do not take it out of its context, but contemplate it in connection with the whole life of Jesus and with the resurrection as well. Otherwise the fixation on the cross, separated from what comes before and after it, truncates the gospel and can lead to serious distortions of our faith.

The death of Jesus on the cross does not come from out of the blue, but results inexorably from his public life, from his words and his deeds. Jesus himself often uses the word "must" when he speaks about his passion. It was clear to him that it had to come this way. "[Jesus] began to teach them [his disciples] that the Son of Man must suffer greatly and be rejected by the elders, the chief priests, and the scribes, and be killed, and rise after three days"(Mk 8:31). After all the suffering is over, Jesus presents that same lesson to the disciples of Emmaus, "Was it not necessary that the Messiah should suffer these things and enter into his glory?" (Lk 24:26). Jesus finds this inevitability foretold by the prophets. The clearest indication is found in the four songs of the servant of Yahweh in Deutero-Isaiah, in which Jesus might have recognized a portrait of his own person and mission. At the baptism in the Jordan, Matthew's gospel makes a direct link to these four songs, because the last verse of his baptism pericope is the first verse of the first song of the servant of Yahweh: "This is my beloved Son, with whom I am well pleased"(Mt 3:17; cf.

Is 42:1; cf. Mt 12:17-21). The servant of Yahweh is sent by God for the salvation of his people; he will suffer much (see especially the fourth song, Is 53), but in this way he will be extremely fruitful, even far beyond the bounds of Israel.

In his baptism, Jesus accepted solidarity with us in our sinfulness. The baptism by John was a baptism for repentance. When Jesus decided to accept this baptism, he consciously and freely chose to share the destiny of people who need repentance. In this way, Jesus opened himself to be infected by human guilt. The incubation period of this disease was three years. In that span of time, the One who did not know sin became sin for our sake, so that we might become in him the righteousness of God (cf. 2 Cor 5:21). That was the passion of Jesus.

In his answer to Pilate, Jesus summarizes with great emphasis his whole mission, "For this I was born and for this I came into the world, to testify to the truth" (Jn 18:37). This is what the life of Jesus was all about: testifying to the truth. Truth, of course, should be understood as the absolute reliability of God's unconditional love. In our world as it happens to be, Jesus has the mission to testify to the truth of God's love and to live it. This is the will of the Father: to convince the people of this love.

Already in the fifth century before Christ, Sophocles in his drama *Antigone* made clear what someone has to expect who wants to love without excluding anyone. Kreon says to his niece, Antigone, "Never an enemy becomes a friend, not even after his death." To this Antigone protests, "Of course he does! I live, not in order to hate, but to love." But Kreon reacts, "Then go to the nether world if you want to love, and there you can love" (vs 522 ff).

The Father did not "will" the crucifixion of his Son; the Father wills only love. The Father wills that his Son should embody the truthfulness and reliability of the divine love, and do so in the real world of ours. Jesus is the Word of the Father made flesh, revealing to us the unfathomable mystery of God: God is love. "But the world did not know him . . . his own people did not accept him" (Jn 1:10-11). It had to happen, according to the terrible logic of this world as we have shaped it. When the rejection of Jesus hardened into passion and then crucifixion, the Father and Son remained faithful and therein revealed the truth and the authenticity of their love. When this happened, the eyes of many people were opened, beginning with the Roman centurion who said, "Truly this man was the Son of God" (Mk 15:39), and continuing with the many who could later proclaim with John, "We have come to know and to believe in the love God has for us" (1 Jn 4:16).

The death of Jesus is not only inseparably connected with his life, it is also profoundly connected with the resurrection. We can only look at the death of Jesus in faith if we do so in the light of the resurrection. That is what the gospels are doing from the very first page. That is also what we call inspiration. On the other hand, if we separate the death of Jesus from the resurrection, our whole Christian faith collapses; then our faith would be in vain and we would still be in our sins (cf. 1 Cor 15:17). The resurrection is the divine confirmation of the whole life of Jesus. There we are shown how infinitely faithful the Father is to the Son and to the message which the Son has brought us. The resurrection opens up the depths of the cross and reveals its real mystery.

Eternal God,
you have invested
your own name and power
in a man, Jesus of Nazareth,
our brother.
But he lived without power
in this world.
You gave him the right to speak—
he is your Word—
but he could not find a hearing.
We ask you
that we may recognize
in him, this man of sorrows,
your first and last Word,
our only savior,
God-with-us,
today and every day
forever and ever.

Twelve

The risen Lord

The first gospel appearance of the risen Lord is to Mary Magdalene, a woman who sought him passionately and faithfully and was the first to be allowed to find him.

To seek and to find: this theme runs like a thread through the whole of scripture. Or more correctly, to be sought and to be found. Because the most important element is not that we seek God, but rather that we let ourselves be found by God and opened up for his presence. I cite here two texts out of the many which illustrate this, one from the Old Testament and one from the New. "When you look for me, you will find me. Yes, when you seek me with all your heart, you will find me with you, says the LORD" (Jer 29:13-14). God himself guarantees this outcome. In the Sermon on the Mount Jesus announces the beatitude, "Blessed are the clean of heart, for they will see God" (Mt 5:8).

This theme of seeking and finding appears frequently in John's gospel. The first word which Jesus speaks in the fourth gospel is not a statement or a challenge, but a question which confronts us in our seeking, "What are you looking for?" (Jn 1:38). At the end of John's gospel, the first word of the risen Lord is, with a small variation, the same question, "Whom are you looking for?" (Jn 20:15). It is the basic

recurring question which Jesus asks each of us. And it is by
no means easy to answer.

In the person of Mary of Magdala this theme of seeking
and finding reaches a unique intensity. She resembles the
bride in the Song of Songs, from which the reading on her
feast is taken:

> On my bed at night I sought him
>   whom my heart loves—
>   I sought him but I did not find him.
> I will rise then and go about the city;
>   in the streets and crossings I will seek
> Him whom my heart loves.
>   I sought him but I did not find him
> (Song of Songs 3:1-2).

She sought him with a passionate dedication and an
unbroken faithfulness. Yet, with all due respect for this great
woman, we must also admit that Mary underestimated Jesus;
the one she seeks is infinitely greater and completely other
than she supposes. She literally seeks the Living among the
dead, the corpse of the Lord who was risen. Her ardent seeking has to be purified, corrected, and above all expanded. This
is not at all a reproach to her. We cannot but think too small
of the Lord. God is always greater than we think he is. Such
underestimation is inescapable for us human beings. But it
helps to be conscious of it.

In our lives, too, seeking and finding God plays a vital
role. It never comes to an end. To find God does not mean
that we do not have to seek him any further. If we find a lost
set of keys, there is, of course, no need to seek any further.
But it is just as obvious that the seeking of God never ceas-
es, because God is always greater and more surprising than
we expect. "In order to be sought after having been found,
God is infinite" (St. Augustine). "Let us seek the Lord in
such a way that we keep seeking him" (St. Bernard of

Clairvaux). God wants our relationship with him to be alive, coming from experience and from the heart. That is why God lures us. "The soul's desire is fulfilled by the very fact of its remaining unsatisfied, for really to see God is never to have had one's fill of desiring God"(St. Gregory of Nyssa). That God communicates God's very self without letting himself be grasped is simultaneously the great pain and the constant stimulus of the mystics. As soon as we cease to seek God with all our heart, our living intimate relationship with God fades. The Revelation of John, the last book of the Bible, speaks about that in its second and third chapter: the danger that we give up our first love, that we become luke-warm. It is not a big, concrete temptation to do something awfully evil, but rather a sneaking, almost imperceptible, but nevertheless fatal erosion. It looks so normal that one hardly notices it, until it is too late. But no, the last remark is not quite correct; it is *never* too late, because the faithfulness of our God is without end.

Thus it is that seeking God goes together with an interior pain. St. Augustine explains this in a homily on the first letter of John (1 Jn 4:6), in a very folksy way:

> The entire life of a good Christian is an exer-cise in holy desire. You do not see what you long for, but the very act of desiring prepares you, so that when God comes you may see and be utterly satisfied. Suppose you are going to fill some holder or container, and you know you will be given a large amount. Then you set about stretching your sack or wineskin or whatever it is. Why? Because you know the quantity you will have to put in it, and your eyes tell you there is not enough room. By stretching it, therefore, you increase the capacity of the sack, and this is how God

deals with us. Simply by making us wait God increases our desire, which in turn enlarges the capacity of our soul, making it able to receive what is to be given to us.

Gregory the Great speaks in a similar vein explicitly about Mary Magdalene:

> Now let us realize what great love had enkindled the heart of this woman: while all the disciples had gone away from the tomb, she just could not leave the spot. She sought him, whom she had not yet found; and while she was seeking him, she wept. And thus it happened that only the one who remained to seek him, did see him. The thrust of every good work is indeed in perseverance, as we heard from the mouth of Truth itself: "whoever perseveres till the end, will be saved" (Mt 10:22). She first sought without finding anything but then she persevered in her seeking and lo and behold, she did find! And thus it happened that her holy desires grew by delay, and that those growing desires eventually found completely what they were looking for.

The unique interplay of seeking and finding in our desire for God does not imply just the ache of inner longing, but also the consolation inherent in knowing we could not seek God if we had not already found God to a certain extent, and if deep down in our heart there were not the certainty that God is longing for this deeper union. From there we draw the strength to persevere.

Focusing more explicitly now on the passage of John 20:11-18, let us begin with the petition that we, too, may seek the Lord with all our heart in faithful perseverance, and that we may find God ever more. St. Ignatius of Loyola advises us wisely to pray for the grace to rejoice intensely *because* of the great glory and joy of Christ Jesus our Lord. It is good to pray for this grace with fervor and perseverance, like the importunate friend (Lk 11) and the persistent widow (Lk 18). Without any hesitation, we can ask for this in Jesus' name, because he promised us three times in a row this fullness of complete joy. (Jn 15:11; 16:24; 17:13). What we pray for is a grace. We cannot produce for ourselves that intense joy which engulfs us totally. By the way, this does not mean that it always has to be a sudden or abrupt joy. It can very well be that this joy grows in us gradually. Above all, we pray to rejoice in *Jesus'* joy and glory; that is to say we pray for the unselfish joy of pure love. This implies that we pray for abiding joy. We pray, as Mother Teresa once put it, that nothing would ever fill us with so much sadness that it could make us forget the joy of the risen Lord. Let us also pray that this joy may permeate all our relationships, so that we shall be able to convey this joy to others in a simple and authentic way.

This passage in John is preceded by the statement that both men—Peter and the other disciple—have gone home, but that Mary Magdalene stayed at the empty tomb. I admire the fidelity and love of this woman, who, like the bride of the Song of Songs, does not count the cost of persevering. And I feel a little uncomfortable with the matter-of-factness of these men. Mary wept while she had lost Jesus. Did that ever move us to tears?

Then come several dialogues. The first one is unambiguous, namely, Mary's conversation with the angels. When they ask why she is weeping, she answers tersely, "They have taken my Lord, and I don't know where they laid him." Indeed, he is her Lord to whom she owes everything and gives herself with an undivided heart. After this brief response, she actually turns her back on the angels. So focused is she on finding Jesus that she is not distracted even by angels!

The second dialogue takes place with the "gardener." She does not know it is Jesus. That happens often with the appearances of the risen Lord. The apostles, the disciples of Emmaus, even Mary Magdalene who loved him so deeply— none of them recognize the risen One. There is a message of faith implied in this blindness. Though it is the same Jesus, he is now completely different. "Death no longer has power over him" (Rom 6:9). He lives a life in which death no longer plays a role. He *lives*, completely other than we live, and also completely other than he lived previously.

The gardener addresses her with the single word, "woman." Mary has become anonymous. She has lost the one who gave her her name and her identity. Then the gardener asks her two questions (thus slipping unnoticed into the role of God, who has the habit of asking questions: "Adam, where are you?" "Cain, where is your brother?" "Simon, son of John, do you love me?") The first question of the gardener makes room for her grief to surface, "Woman, why are you weeping?" What a profound question. It touches Mary in the depth of her heart and is the first step toward healing. The questioner expresses sincere concern for her. That gives her the opportunity to speak about her grief, to articulate it, to share it.

The second question, "Whom are you looking for?" goes even deeper. It is *the* question of John's gospel. It is about her (and our) deepest desire, about her (and our) most profound relationship. The hope of the evangelist, John, is that the honest answer to this question will be: "Jesus." His whole gospel was written "that you may come to believe that Jesus is the Messiah, the Son of God, and that through this belief you may have life in his name" (Jn 20:31). In Mary this hope was fulfilled. Though her love must still be purified and expanded, she really seeks Jesus with an unabashedly passionate desire. Her whole-hearted answer shows whom she is looking for, "Sir, if you carried him away, tell me where you laid him, and I will take him."

Then comes the encounter. The risen Lord calls her forth from her anonymity, from her burning emptiness, from her too-narrow vision. He calls her into the new reality opened up by Jesus' resurrection from the dead. He calls her by her name, and does so from beyond the boundary of death. He calls her as his Father had once called Israel, "Fear not, for I have redeemed you; I have called you by name: you are mine" (Is 43:1).

He calls her like the good shepherd who calls his own sheep by name and leads them out (Jn 10:3). He calls her by her old name which went with him through death and resurrection and thus has become new, sharing in the glory of the new life over which death has no power any more. He calls her by her name, "Mary!" and thus seals an intimacy that is unique. "I shall also give a white amulet upon which is inscribed a new name, which no one knows except the one who receives it" (Rev 2:17; cf. Is. 62:2).

Jesus knows whom he calls. He knows her past and her story. He knows her guilt and her anguish, her love and her hope. He knows her fully, far better than she knows herself. When Jesus pronounces her name, it encompasses the fullness which omits nothing and includes everything. In this fullness she is called and loved. In this love everything is taken up, everything finds its place. She does not need to hold back anything, to hide anything, or to repress anything. She meets the love of the risen Lord who knows no limits and sets no conditions.

> The LORD, your God, is in your midst,
>   a mighty savior;
> He will rejoice over you with gladness,
>   and renew you in his love.
> He will sing joyfully because of you,
>   as one sings at festivals (Zep 3:17-18).

When Jesus in this way calls her by her name, an unheard of liberation and change takes place in Mary Magdalene. Her grief and pain disappear like snow before the sun, yes, even faster and more radical. She is able to open herself completely, she can surrender herself, she is filled with a fullness of joy. In the one word *Rabbouni* she expresses all this. She experiences the complete and radical transition into a new life that stands before her in the person of Jesus and is given to her through him. She receives her name—and herself—completely renewed.

The encounter between Jesus and Mary Magdalene is unique and ineffable. Yet, at the same time, something takes place here that is meant for each of us. We are all addressed in this way by the risen Lord and thus led into a new life. Francois Varillon, S.J., summarized this invitation and its link to our own transformation :

> Christ is risen,
> therefore alive,
> therefore present,
> therefore active,
> therefore transforming,
> therefore making us divine.

This is true for each of us. In his resurrection Jesus enables us "to be conformed to his image" (cf. Rom 8:29). From this point further John's saying holds with a new intensity, "We should be called children of God; and that is what we are." (1 Jn 3:1 NRSV).

The appearances of the risen Lord all lead into a mission. Whoever has really encountered him must testify of him and spread the news of the resurrection. Such an experience one cannot hold for oneself. Mary of Magdala is no exception. In her great love she does not want to lose the one whom she sought with so much anguish and fidelity. She must learn, however, that true union with Jesus consists not in clinging to him, but in letting ourselves be sent out in his name to our brothers and sisters. Possessiveness is the greatest danger in love. Even the most pure love has to learn this through much pain. "Stop holding on to me . . . but go to my brothers and sisters and tell them. . . ."

Jesus, who had called Mary by her name and awakened her to a new life, now also entrusts to her his mission. He confides to her the message, "I am going to my Father and your Father. . . ." In these words Jesus captures the fulfillment of his own mission. He came to us in order to usher us into the mystery in which he, himself, dwells: his oneness with the Father in the Holy Spirit. That is the most intimate and precious gift he can share with us. This mystery is the source of all love, of all life, and of all fruitfulness. We, too, are invited to be at home and rooted in this mystery. "Remain in my love" (Jn 15:9). We are no longer slaves, full of fear, but we received the Spirit who makes us into children of God and lets us cry out, "Abba, Father!" (cf. Rom 8:15).

When the Father of Jesus is also our Father, then we are all brothers and sisters, "There is neither Jew nor Greek, there is neither slave nor free person, there is not male and female; for you are all one in Christ Jesus" (Gal 3:28). For our day and age—with its many refugees, its dismissal of aliens, and its cruel violence—this is a very timely message and challenge.

"Mary of Magdala went and announced to the disciples, 'I have seen the Lord.'" St. Augustine, St. Bernard of Clairvaux, and other doctors of the church call Mary Magdalene with delight, *apostola apostolorum*, the apostle of the apostles. She brought to the apostles the core of the good news, its ultimate confirmation and completion. In the Middle Ages there was a very popular collection of legends of the saints, written by the Dominican Jacobus de Voragine under the title, *Golden Legends*. His book relates with great, great imagination and warmth how Mary radiated with her whole person this message of Jesus. Before she was even able to utter a word, her whole being had conveyed the joy of the resurrection. During his long illness in 1521, this was one of the two books which Ignatius of Loyola read. It made a lasting and deep impression on him. His advice to pray for the grace to rejoice intensely over the great glory and joy of Christ Jesus our Lord might have its origin in this story.

In being sent to the disciples, Mary herself made a very important discovery. In her mission she experienced intimate union with Jesus. What she had tried earlier to achieve herself by holding on to Jesus was now given as a pure gift in the mission she carried out. She was sent by Jesus, and in this mission he was close to her, much closer than in the garden by the tomb. In her mission she was privileged to experience what St. Paul later will say about himself, "I live, no longer I, but Christ lives in me" (Gal 2:20). The true union is not in feelings or words, but in the mission toward the people, in the service of everyday life.

Teresa of Avila describes in her book, *The Interior Castle*, the growth of prayer life. She distinguishes seven phases or stages, which she describes as seven mansions located increasingly further in the castle of the soul. Using this analogy of the seven mansions, she treats at great length the experiences of prayer and mysticism. The seventh and last mansion stands for the highest mystical union. This, too, she describes in a powerful way. Then, however, a most unexpected turn suddenly comes: whoever reaches the seventh mansion finds himself or herself back on the street.

The thirteenth-century Flemish mystic, Hadewych, refers to a similar experience. In her fifth vision, she describes the bliss of the highest possible union with God: "An ecstasy which transcends all understanding," which, however, abruptly passes into the divine command, "return to your work." The fact that Jesus entrusts to us his mission seals our union with him. "'As the Father has sent me, so I send you.' And when he had said this, he breathed on them and said to them, 'Receive the holy Spirit'" (Jn 20:21-22).

We have received the grace to know and to rejoice that in our mission today the risen Jesus lives and works in us, just as the Father lived and worked in Jesus when he walked this earth.

We worship and admire you, God,
because you have shown your power
in Jesus Christ,
raising him from the dead
and setting him at your right hand,
exalting him above all powers
and giving him a name
which is above every name in this world.
We ask you
that we who believe in him
may be of his mind as well,
that we may be a sign
of his life,
light and peace to all
who seek you,
today and every day
forever and ever.

Notes

Chapter 1

1. *Open Secret*, translated by John Moyne and Coleman Barks (Putney, VT: Threshold Books, 1984), p.50.

2. cf. Monika Hirschauer et. al., *Gott finden im Alltag. Exerzitien zu Hause* (Freiburg i. Br., Germany: Herder, 1998), p.9.

3. Cf. Peter Koester and Herman Andriessen, *Sein Leben ordnen* (Freiburgi., Br., Germany: Herder, 1991), p. 31.

Chapter 2

1. Kathleen Norris. *Amazing Grace* (New York: Riverhead Books, 1998), p.150.

2. Blaise Arminjon, S.J., *Sur la lyre a dix cordes* (Paris: DDB, 1990), p. 131.

3. Cf. *Kleines Kirchenjahr* (Muenchen: Ars sacra, 1954), pp. 15-19.

4. Most of the concluding prayers are taken from Huub Oosterhuis, *Your Word Is Near: Contemporary Christian Prayers*, translated by N.D. Smith (New York, N.Y.: Paulist Press 1968)

Chapter 6

1. This paragraph is inspired by remarks of Card. Carlo M. Martini on the vital areas where the growth or decline of the sense of mission ordinarily takes place. See his book *Uomini di Pace e di Reconciliazione* (Roma: Edizioni Borla, 1985), Sesta Meditatione.

2. Barbara Hallensleben, who coined this expression, was the first to write an extensive, thorough and very inspiring "Theology of

Mission" (in German: *Theologie der Sendung*, Frankfurt am Main, 1994). She is now professor of systematic theology at the University of Fribourg, Switzerland.

Chapter 8

1. Cf. *One Minute Wisdom* (Garden City, N.Y.: Doubleday, 1968), p. 206.

2. Cf. Max Frisch, *Tagebuch* (Muenchen-Zuerich, 1965), p. 26ff.

Chapter 9

1. Quote taken from pp. 66-68, *Jesus: The Gift of Love* by Jean Vanier. Copyright © 1994. All rights reserved. Used with permission of the Crossroad Publishing Company, New York.

2. Sabine Naegeli, *Die Nacht ist voller Sterne* (Freiburg i. Br., Germany: Herder, 1997), p. 82f.

Chapter 10

1. *The Gift of Peace* (Chicago: Loyola Press, 1997), p. 51. After an exemplary life of service to God's people, Cardinal Bernardin of Chicago was falsely accused by Steven Cook and his lawyer of sexual abuse. Later the charges were rescinded.

2. Sabine Naegeli, *Die Nacht ist voller Sterne* (Freiburg i. Br., Germany: Herder, 1997), p. 80f.

Chapter 11

1. Sabine Naegeli, *Die Nacht ist voller Sterne* (Freiburg i. Br., Germany: Herder, 1997), p. 106f.